THE DAY AFTER TOMORROW

This catalogue was published with the support of the Expo'98,

on the occasion of the exhibition presented in the Centro Cultural de Belém

by Lisboa 94

20 September - 18 December 1994

THE DAY AFTER TOMORROW

CENTRO CULTURAL DE BELÉM

Lisboa
Capital
Europeia da
Cultura '94

Electa

CENTRO
CULTURAL
DE BELÉM

LISBOA 94

CHAIRMAN
Vítor Constâncio

ADVISERS
PRESS, PUBLIC RELATIONS AND PROTOCOL
Maria Nobre Franco

Jorge Pires

Fernando Camecelha

Tomás Collares Pereira

Leonor Vaz

INTERNATIONAL RELATIONS
Ivonne Cunha Rego

ASSISTANT
Graça Maria Contreiras

EXHIBITIONS
DIRECTOR
Simonetta Luz Afonso

ADVISERS
Isabel Carlos

Raffaella D'Intino

Paulo Pereira

ASSISTANTS
Clara de Gubernatis

Paula Santos

PRODUCTION
Maria Amélia Ferreira da Silva

EDITION
António Martins

CLASSICAL MUSIC AND OPERA
LITERATURE AND THINKING
DIRECTOR
José Carlos Megre

ADVISERS
CLASSICAL MUSIC AND OPERA
Manuel Pedro Ferreira

Maria José Rino

Teresa Castanheira

LITERATURE AND THINKING
Graça Vasconcelos

Rosa Midões Domingues

ASSISTANT
André Cordeiro

THEATRE AND DANCE
ADMINISTRADORA / DIRECTOR
Maria Manuel Pinto Barbosa

ADVISERS
Jorge Salavisa

Margarida Lages

Teresa Reimão Pinto

Elsa Marques

CINEMA AND VIDEO
DIRECTOR
Ana Costa Almeida

ADVISERS
Maria Miguel Santos Silva

Antónia Seabra

ENTERTAINMENT, POPULAR MUSIC AND EDITIONS
DIRECTOR
Ruben de Carvalho

ADVISERS
Helena Costa

Modesto Navarro

Inês Mota

URBAN INTERVENTION
DIRECTOR
Elísio Summavielle

ADVISERS
Gonçalo Couceiro

Maria José Machado Santos

Helena Caria

PROMOTION
ADMINISTRADOR / DIRECTOR
José Luís Arnaut

ADVISERS
Rita Gallo

Sofia Costa Pessoa

Cláudia Gomes da Silva

GENERAL MANAGEMENT AND SPONSOR RELATIONS
DIRECTOR
Adelaide Rocha

ADVISERS
Miguel Lobo Antunes

João Nascimento

Paula Martins Guerreiro

Paula Catita

ASSISTANT
Maria Carrelhas

Printed in Italy

© 1994 by Lisboa 94

and by Electa, Milan

Elemond Editori Associati

EXHIBITION

LISBOA 94

EXECUTIVE COMMITTEE

DIRECTOR
Simonetta Luz Afonso

ADVISERS
Isabel Carlos
Raffaella D'Intino
Paulo Pereira

EXECUTIVE ASSISTANT
Clara de Gubernatis

PRODUCTION
Maria Amélia Ferreira da Silva
Paula Santos

FUNDAÇÃO DAS DESCOBERTAS
CENTRO CULTURAL DE BELÉM

BOARD OF DIRECTORS

PRESIDENT
Carlos Antero Ferreira

VOGAL
Teresa Ferreira Lima

VOGAL
Maria José Stock

EXHIBITION CENTER

DIRECTOR
José de Monterroso Teixeira

TEMPORARY EXHIBITIONS DEPARTMENT

CURATORS
Rita Lougares
Isabel Penha Garcia

EDITORIAL DEPARTMENT
Alexandra Araújo
Gonçalo Bènard-Guedes

DOCUMENTATION DEPARTMENT
Luísa Bernardino

PUBLIC RELATIONS
Maria da Conceição Simões de Almeida

CURATOR
Isabel Carlos

EXECUTIVE CURATOR
Isabel Carlos

ARCHITECTURAL PROJECT
Rui Orfão

SETTING
Coutinho & Coutinho

LIGHTING
António Ribeiro

TRANSPORTS
Maertens I.T.

ACKNOWLEGEMENTS

All the artists featured in this exhibition.

Institutions and private collectors who lent works from their collections:
Contemporary Art Society, London; Georges Guilbaud, Janet de Botton, McGuinness-Finch.

Special supports granted by:
EC Japan Festival, Goethe-Institut Lissabon.

All those who committed themselves to this exhibition:

Alexandra Araújo, Alice Wohl, Amèlie Darras, António Portela, AR.CO, Câmara Municipal de Lisboa, Centro Cultural de Belém, Direcção Geral dos Edifícios e Monumentos Nacionais, EC Japan Festival, Gilda Williams, Goethe-Institut Lissabon, Graça Costa Cabral, Greg Hilty, Hans Winterberg, Helena Abrantes, IPPAR, Iria Caetano, Isabel Penha Garcia, João Cayatte, José Canas, José Teixeira, Mafalda Magalhães Barros, Marco Aurélio, Marianna Baer, Maria José Stock, Maureen Burns, Merle Jubelin, Metropolitano de Lisboa E.P., Michael Bond, Ministério das Obras Públicas e Comunicações, Museu Nacional de Etnologia (Lisbon), Patrícia Vieira, Paulo Varela Gomes, Rita Lougares, RN Trans (Mr. Branco and team), Shugi Kogi, Susan Brades, Tóbis, Valentim de Carvalho, Vasco Costa, Vitória Mesquita.

To museums and private galleries:

Galerie Bernd Klüser, Munich; Galerie Jennifer Flay, Paris; Galerie Marc Jancou, Zurich; Mori Gallery, Sydney; Sandra Gering Gallery, New York; Shiraishi Contemporary Art Inc., Tokyo; The Henry Moore Sculpture Trust, England; The Israel Museum, Jerusalem; Sean Kelly, New York.

CATALOGUE

AUTHORS

Isabel Carlos

José Jiménez

António Sena

João Fernandes

Alexandre Melo

Akira Asada

Rui Eduardo Paes

Andrew Renton

Jonathan Watkins

António Cerveira Pinto

Michael Archer

Julia Brown Turrell (Ed.)

Helmut Friedel

TRANSLATION

David Alan Prescott

Nigel Thomas

James Ormiston

Helen Domachowski

Francisco José Magalhães

Richard Sams

PHOTOGRAPHY

António Pinto

Laura Castro Caldas and Paulo Cintra

José Pessoa (Arquivo Nacional de Fotografia)

Lado Mlekuz

Darin Pappas

John Riddy

Francisco Alcantara

Mario Gastinger

Victor Arnolds

J. Linders

Gorlich / Metzel

André Kosters (IN SITU)

EDITORIAL COORDINATION

António Martins

Raffaella D'Intino

TEXTS REVIEW

James Ormiston

Paula Santos

ART DIRECTOR

Henrique Cayatte

GRAFIC DESIGN

António Lobo

COLOUR SELECTION AND PRINTING

Electa

EDITION

Electa-Lisboa 94

CONTENTS

FOREWORD

Contemporary art is a permanent challenge. That is what makes it enthralling. Its mobility of invention, the strength of current creation, the great circuits of circulation, commercialization and public showing of the artists' works implies an effort of accompanying which is demanded by all those who deal with art. The very velocity of the cycles of taste and their acceleration are other motifs of seduction of the technique of contemporary art, especially given the existence of diverse centres of production and the growing importance of that which was previously called "the off-centre".

It is also worth stating that today — particularly today — there are no excuses for contemporary art, in its diversity, in its multiplicity of means of expression and content, not being part of the cultural background either of the specialists (none of them should ignore it) or the general public (which should gradually be getting familiar with it).

Within the Area of the Exhibition Section for Lisbon 94, European Capital of Culture *Depois de Amanhã (The Day After Tomorrow)*, presented in the Centro Cultural de Belém, has been, since its beginning — I may say since the first preparatory meetings for the whole event —, an absolute priority, aiming at integrating Portugal within the international circuit of contemporary plastic creation by means of a great international show. But not only international. One should stress the preponderant role played by the Portuguese artists in the presentation of completely unknown projects, accompanied in this by their foreign colleagues, some of whom (the vast majority) have never been on show among us and who are displaying here works produced totally for Lisbon 94. The previously unknown nature of the works and their quality are factors which should move a public which, for reasons of the tradition of consumption, has not welcomed contemporaneity as much as we would like, despite the role played both by public and private institutions, which proves that it is necessary to do much more in this field if we wish to create a past for our future…

Now that Lisbon has a multiplicity of cultural facilities, the fact that this exhibition is the starting point for the recognition of Lisbon as one of the European poles for the presenting of contemporary art is already, more than a desire, a certainty.

From the outset we considered the Centro Cultural de Belém as an ideal partner for the realizing of this project, and we hereby wish to express our gratitude to the following for their collaboration: Professor Antero Ferreira, Professor Maria José Stock, and Dr José Teixeira, as well as the whole team of the Exhibition Module.

Simonetta Luz Afonso

Instituto Português de Museus Director
Lisboa 94 Exhibitions Director

INTRODUCTION

This exhibition shows, for the first time in Lisbon, a series of works which have been projected and created in the Portuguese context.

Also, the desired encounter between local and foreign artists derives from the simultaneous desire to slowly introduce Lisbon into an international route of contemporary art, besides trying to establish a showing in which there is a crossing not only of languages, but also of clearly established generations and names with others who are still in the process of affirming themselves.

Heterogeneity and plurality were criteria. But, now at the end of the process, I think that it is clear that there are common traits running through the works, even because, with greater or smaller differences, we all live in the same world and on the same planet. I will only mention those that seem obvious to me: the problematics of the body (Miguel Ângelo Rocha, Cathy de Monchaux, Julião Sarmento); the work (and re-elaboration) of the modernist inheritance (Ângela Ferreira); the relationship between art and technology (Taro Chiezo), among other no less important problematics in the field of the modern condition (the continuity of the exploring of traditional supports as a valid and compulsive research). In the same way, photography (Thiel, Alves da Silva) was not taken here in its purist (and up to a point self-segregating) sense: it was rather considered as another artistic support, just like painting, sculpture, video or music, being able to show and tell.

From the beginning this project also had a component in the area of urban extension, in strict collaboration with the Goethe Institut, namely Mr Hans Winterberg, who was the co-Curator of the programme for the Terreiro do Paço, supporting the works of Stephan Balkenhol, Olaf Metzel, and Marie Jo Lafontaine (the latter presenting her work in the indoor exhibition facilities but with a work that should be read out in connection with the urban installations, as it is based on the same presuppositions and realities as the works of Balkenhol and Metzel).

All this has been done so that we don't die of truth (as Nietzsche would say).

Isabel Carlos

Exhibition Curator

OF THE NEED TO SEE

Isabel Carlos

1. History teaches us that the state of affairs at the end of a century carries a certain "ar du temps" and that during this period certain pre-eminent and more or less serious questions are posed. One of them is the question of the *end*, an inflated word in these recent times, particularly in relation to the artistic field. It is the end of painting, it is the end of the museum, it is the end of history, it is the end of criticism. But then painting carries on, art carries on being made, museums are still built and essays and critiques are still written. One then concludes that the end of these "things" is not something that can be decreed and stipulated.

The reason, amongst many, obviously, may lie in a certainty, which someone we may consider as one of the first of the moderns, the French architectural theorist Antoine Chrysostome known as Quatremère de Quincy (1755-1849), formulated at the beginning of the 19th Century in the following way: "On a souvent demandé quelles furent les causes morales de la grande perfection des Arts en Grèce. A cela, il y a une réponse qui, si elle ne comprend pas toutes ces causes, en renferme au moins un très-grand nombre. On peut, ce me semble, répondre d'un seul mot, que la supériorité ou la perfection qu'obtinrent les Grecs en cette partie, fut due à ce que chez eux les arts étaient *nécessaires*.

Nécessaire peut s'entendre ici sous plus d'un sens et se dire de plus d'une manière.

Si l'on parle des Arts, en les considérant dans leur génération et dans leur propriété qu'ils ont de se produire, de se perpétuer d'eux-mêmes sans aucun secours étranger, *nécessaire* signifie *obligé, forcé d'être*[1]. Upon this notion which states the existence of art as rooted in necessity, in other words, the works of art exist because they are originaly necessary — as is then made explicit — they are necessary because they are *obligatory*, forced into *being*, is one of the most convincing and true explanations as to why there is art and why it is true that while Man exists there will always be art. Because, these "things" are intrinsicaly "necessary" for us, they have to be and have to happen, they are compulsory and obligatory and there are even people who are addicted to art or art-dependent (whom we call, in the art world, artists, critics, curators). What I am trying to show, is art's inevitability and its indispensable condition: "...peut-on mieux proclamer l'inutilité des ouvrages de l'Art, qu'en annonçant dans les recueils qu'on en fait la nullité de leur emploi. Les enlever tous indistinctement à leur destination sociale, qu'est-ce autre chose, sinon dire que la société n'en a pas besoin? Et cependant, par une contradiction singulière, on prétend que c'est pour l'avantage des Arts et des artistes. Mais quel est donc cet avantage des artistes et des arts, qui n'est pas l'intérêt de la société? Les uns et les autres n'existent-ils pas pour elle et par elle?"[2]. Art exists for and due to society and that will be the way as long as there are human beings: yesterday, today, tomorrow, and *the day after tomorrow*.

2. The title of this exhibition, one should remember, appears within this context; it doesn't mean a desire to point out tendencies, to announce futures, to state that art is going this or that way; but merely to escape from the catastrophism, the teleological and apocalyptical state of affairs in which we live in a certain way nowadays. And then to do it not through exclusion but through *inclusion*, through seeking out the various artistic languages that today exist side by side in the field of art instead of searching for a segment or a certain line: heterogeneity as a criterion for the choice and selection of artists and works.

This exhibition aims towards a flight from purism and from a restricting vision, which does not necessarily mean a defence of impurity and contamination, but merely the recognition of plurality, of the differences and the non-hierarchical nature of the languages: perhaps this is the most radically new thing that our end of century has to offer and carry out, unlike previous periods in which "The fundamental impulse toward both homogeneity and the segregation of opposites emerged from the opprobrium attached to unclassifiable mixtures. From a regulatory standpoint, heterogeneity was dangerous because it nakedly coupled, and thereby undermined dichotomies"[3]. And even though heterogeneity may continue to be considered dangerous or carry within it some sort of weakness, disfunctionality, or may even be accused of lacking any firm and fast idea, it is absolutely necessary. Because we believe, like Foucault[4], that critical discourse exists in the flaws, in the chinks of other discourses, as the problem is that of keeping a critical distance, not only outside the language, but also within it, without postulating another overall theory of the language. Any form of critical discourse which does not experience its instability and disorder is immediately confronted with its limitations. So one mustn´t look, in this text or in this exhibition, for certainties and formulae for the understanding of contemporary art. I don't have them and I don't want to have them.

Naturally, more than in "evolution" or "progress", I believe that the artistic territory operates in *deepening* and *radicalization*, through a "revealing" of another angle, that is through shifting, insistence,or disrupting the rules, according to the creative circumstances or the respective contexts. A deepening, when what is at issue is the use of apparently exhausted expressive supports, but which nevertheless still constitute an artistic corpus from which current aesthetic and plastic problems may be raised (see, for example, the painting of Pedro Calapez and his relationship with Piranesi, now shown with references to the modern inheritance of monochromatism...). Radicalization, when one bends a certain language to the limit, whether plastic or communicational, issuing forth messages which are sometimes socially or politically orientated or suspending the possibility of judgement (for example, with João Paulo Feliciano, interweaving a day-to-day object, removed from its context, with rock music, between experimentation and derision).

From this point of view I stray from Adorno and his theory of advanced materials — which made him see, for example, the returning to figuration as an impossibility — and I draw closer to Burger's notion, which harks back to Friedrich Schlegel, and according to which each work of art itself establishes the "critical" criterion by which it must be analysed. This is not imposed from outside: on the contrary, it is intrinsic to it[5].

The Day After Tomorrow, to get back to the title of this exhibition, also in the sense given to it by Álvaro de Campos — one of the heteronyms of the Portuguese poet Fernando Pessoa: "Só depois de amanhã... / Hoje quero preparar-me para pensar amanhã no dia seguinte" (Only after tomorrow... / Today I want to prepare myself to think about the next day tomorrow). Not as an "Adiamento" (Putting off), the title of the poem from which these words were taken — but rather the need for a stop to look, if possible, *Seeing without charting*.

This exhibition, more than playing with the drawing up of a chart of current contemporary art, aims at — to continue the geographical analogy — providing a little *compass*, from which one may depart in different directions and on different paths. There is no certainty at the beginning, the map is absent, only the discovery and the surprise of the discovery can happen. One is only following a given direction, ignoring the final destination, ignoring the territory. To see and chart is the most usual practice today, when faced with contemporary art: before the work of art one looks about more (and in parallel) than one looks at it. Actually, one reads more than one sees. That we make of this the very object of artistic work, turning the atitude into the work of art itself, is what makes a work like that by Narelle Jubelin so sublimely intelligent and interesting. Only that here, cartography is strictly metaphor.

This attitude which radically leads to an invisibility, to a blindness — as Andrew Renton states — is ultimately the greatest defence of Seeing, an inner Seeing, a reflective seeing, of research and knowledge, "the eye and the spirit", as Merleau-Ponty would say. Another issue which we sometimes tend to forget, as we live in a world invaded by images, is that to see it is necessary to know. It is not enough to see, and artistic and visual illiteracy really exist.

Barbara Stafford precisely diagnoses the situation we live in today: "As we approach our own fin-de-siècle, how can we remedy the unproductive attitude that places a wedge between the 'substantial' sciences and the 'insubstantial' humanities, or divorces 'high' ratiocination from 'merely manual' and miracle-mongering technology? [...] But, to paraphrase Gauguin, who are we imagists and, more to the point, where are we going? Consider a different, cross — and pluridisciplinary viewpoint, one in which there is a profound interplay between observation and theory. More necessary than interaction, however, is a fundamental reorientation"[6]. Such a reorientation seems to take place with the simultaneously physical and metaphysical works of James Turrell: see, in his installation, the substantial technology and rigour creating the insubstantial light which transports us to the limits of our perception and of our bodies.

As an art critic I have always defended a radical returning to Seeing. Seeing, rather than just looking, is indispensable, and it is easy to find works in this exhibition which play within the visibility taken to its extreme (Delvoye, Xana). Works which openly demand and oppose the erasing of the image and of the respective visual charge, or which even problematize matters of perception (João Penalva). I leave the possibility of discovering these two axes to the viewer whilst wandering through the exhibition, amongst the works by all the artists, and not only among these that may stand out because they are mentioned within the parentheses of a text.

I completely accept the game of our contemporary condition: the visual as the most efficient way of communicating. The awareness of this reality has the most interesting practices at its extreme point whether in the game of the excess of visibility, in powerful image machines; or in the game of invisibility, in the infra-image. I thus place myself, in this exhibition, on a level which derives from a practice: that of an *art critic*. And as such, more than as a Curator who provides clues in this text as to the works on show — I leave that to the texts in this catalogue written on each artist, or not written due to the choice of the artist himself (the case of Pedro Cabrita Reis and Julião Sarmento) — I prefer to reflect upon the place of criticism, even because I think that such a reflexion will reveal choices and stand-points. Effectively, more than explaining works of art, considering their problematics of communication, I am much more interested in talking about them, to discourse without exercising a unilateral authority which reduces the possibility of interpretation, and even the error of interpretation or, why not, lack of understanding: because this is the unavoidable condition of art in the new modern state of affairs.

3. Criticism is one of the founding concepts of modernity. In the 18th century, criticism establishes itself as a new literary genre: as a controversial mediating agent between the works and the public.

Kant, with his *Critique of Judgement*, no longer sees aesthetics as an appendix of moral philosophy and consecrates it as a discipline of reflection on taste, as a theorization of sensitive perfection; finally, as a critique of the judgement of aesthetics.

In this work we thus find the notion that the aesthetic idea cannot become knowledge, because it is an intuition (of the imagination), an intuition through which we will never be able to find an adequate concept. Thus, the judgement of taste is based on a universality (just as the judgement of logic), but on a subjective universality, as it is unknowable and undemonstrable.

The dice were thus cast for a reflection which the history of thought has never since abandoned. Walter Benjamin, in the work which deals with the concept of aesthetical criticism in German Romanticism, defines criticism as a type of experimentation on the work of art, going on to state: "...devrait-il exister des journaux critiques qui traitent les auteurs selon une technique médicale et chirurgicale, et ne se contentent pas de dépister la maladie et de la notifier avec un malin plaisir"[7]. Not being content with diagnosing the disease and pointing it out with malicious pleasure. Because — and it is this that Benjamin in a sense defends here — criticism should be like a 'technique' at the service of art"[8].

Miguel Baptista Pereira makes this concept clearer by showing the evolution of the term criticism: "Whereas in the judicial, theological and medical context the word 'crisis' had the meaning of a decision, the term 'criticism' lost its initial exclusive link to 'crisis' and became applied to the art or technique of judging with the emphasis on its gnoseological structure". He goes on: "The initial dominance of the aesthetic explains not only the special use of the word 'criticism' to describe the method of investigating the phenomenon of the beautiful, the knowledge of it and its production, but also E. Cassirer's interpretation, which subordinates the 'critical epoch' to the viewpoint of the fundamental problems of Aesthetic and establishes a union between philosophy and art criticism"[8]. Curiously, in Adorno, the term technique keeps on appearing intrinsically connected to the term criticism. This thinker states: "The technique is the determinable figure of the enigma in works of art, a figure which is both rational and abstract. It authorizes judgement in the zone which is deprived of judgement"[9].

This essential problem ("judgement in the zone which is deprived of judgement") is the fulcrum to consider in relation to a reflection on the relationship between art and art criticism. Is a discourse on art possible? It is not, in itself, an area which constantly escapes naming and designation? Or is art, merely, a phenomenon of naming?

Thierry de Duve begins his book *Au Nom de l'Art*[10] with an ingenious metaphor: that of the Martian who lands on our planet and tries to understand what "this thing" that the earthlings call "art" is. A metaphor which immediately establishes the dimension of the "other", of the strange and unfamiliar. Or rather, Duve puts the Foucaultian problematization into action: the Other is caught up in a relationship of dependency or derivation from the Same and it is when the familiar becomes unfamiliar that thought is forced to question itself and to face alternatives for itself. For Foucault, critical thought is born precisely from this non-recognition, this warped mirror — to use an image which was dear to him[11] — in which the confrontation with the radical alterity forces this critical thought to see itself.

In fact, Duve's "Martian" has all of Duve's own criticisms. Therefore there are sentences like "...vous avez été à l'école structuraliste d'un Lévi-Strauss martien, plus prestigieuse sur votre planète..."[12]; or other sentences like that he offers when faced with the "Martian's" unconvincedness, after having been through all the theories on art, from sociological to semiological, going through the avant-garde ones: "vous êtes en réalité, ou un idéaliste aveugle ou un cynique invétéré"[13]. And through the Martian's "gaze", it is in this way that Duve concludes that this art is halfway between magic and scientific knowledge[14] and that art is everything that men call art[15], a nominalist strategy which shapes all of his work. The confrontation with Nicolau de Cusa's theory of negative theology is almost inevitable. According to this medieval philosopher, the only thing we can say about God is that He is not, as He is so completely different to humans; well, art, in Duve's way of seeing it, is, on the contrary, precisely that which we say is art, that which we call art, not ceasing to be something that it isn't until the injunction which defines it as such takes place, no matter what the chosen object is: only that we are now on the profane side, and the nominalism serves a strategy of naming a family of objects produced by man: necessary, because it has to be...

And in this context the figure of the critic is insurmountable: "Avec le statut professionnel viennent évidemment un pouvoir, une tribune, une autorité professorale exercée dans l'enseignement ou les medias, une expertise réelle ou supposée, un charisme éventuel et des possibilités d'user d'influence sur le public, voire de manipuler le marché. Mais ce n'est pas le pouvoir qui devrait faire le critique, c'est sa réputation, et celle-ci s'impose en s'exposant. La critique d'art, en publiant ses jugements, demande à être jugée sur la qualité de ceux-ci et s'en remet par necessité au veredict de l'avenir"[16].

If for Duve the quality of the critic is subject to the verdict of the future, for Lyotard certain forms of art have moved beyond the critical phase and demand more from critical discourse than the majority of the discriminatory concepts of criticism. Just as Hegel announced "the end of art", Lyotard announces "the end of all criticism"[17]. Art moves beyond critical discourse and, on a certain level, even moves on a different path in which it does not incorporate criticism: it jumps out of it and remains totally beyond it.

This post-critical condition can even be taken as an "end of aesthetics" because this art places itself not only beyond criticism but also beyond that which is traditionally considered art. Lyotard's reflection thus appears to us as one of the signs of the contradictory status of aesthetics in general.

One of the limit areas between criticism and art is the discourse on painting. A first reason we may evoke for such a fact is the use of extremely diverse codes: if a critique of a literary work is situated after all within the same signs (linguistic signs), the same is not true in relation to painting (or sculpture, as well), where the signs, being visual, also belong to (or refer back to) other continents of experience and of knowledge. Language, communication and discourse on the one hand, and form, colour and visual figures (that is art like painting, or rather depicting) on the other. The problem facing the critic is how to go "beyond" language *using* language. The same sense is shared by Foucault when he points out the principle of radical discontinuity between the visual and the discoursive, evoking the infinite potential of the game of depicting in painting[18].

One may then begin from the principle that the main enemy of art in general is theoretical discourse (Lyotard), because it limits — if not represses — alterity, incorporating what is not systematical within the system. The critic should thus risk the safety of his knowledge and the satisfaction of appropriation and "discovery" in favour of intensity, insecurity, disruption and transgression. But never forgetting that the aim of the philosopher-critic is not to become an artist, but to indicate the *exterior nature* of his discourse[19].

These lines and this reflection on art and art criticism intend to cast some light on the exterior nature which always exists inevitably in the discourse on art. Even because it is not only theory that is exterior to art, but the theory itself "is founded" in an exteriority. The issue, furthermore, is that the word-theory has invaded artistic territory more and more: "A paradox of our supposedly uneducated media culture is that it remains an heir to the overestimation of written language. From the Neoclassical diagram, or universal, stripped-down 'characteristic', to the Romantic grammar of chemical elements, or to the Cubists' punning words and eleborate letters, to Conceptual Art's decontextualized inscriptions, to Jenny Holzer's terse captions — texts, charts, definitions, and documentation increasingly turned graphics into linguistics"[20]. However, as Marcel Proust once noted, a work in which the theories are still there is like an object with the price tag still on.

4. What is a fact is that there is a new relationship with the real, which leads us to suggest a new word for the world of today's images: more than depicting, many contemporary works of art act within a *presentification*. The works of Miguel Palma or Baltazar Torres act precisely within a presentification of realities more than any exercise of staging or representation, they presentify so that we can see what we look at every day.

Another question which has been imposed by the modernist rupture is that art has stopped being incorporated within the sacred (Middle Ages) and has placed itself *in the place of* the sacred. All the statements and defences of "art for art's sake" are a symptom of this: they are true theologies of art. Thus it is not surprising that museums have been acquiring a more and more circumstantial and devout character, becoming today's cathedrals.

The presentification as a contemporary status of art, more than ever, reveals a type of no place, of between-place, of *interior indecision* towards the artistic language itself: something which justifies and imposes the recognition that only heterogeneity justifies a curatorial approximation to the artists' work. If criticism itself, as we have seen, acts within a between-space, if the works themselves appear as objects in the "open" world, the choice of works of art arises from the becoming aware of this impossibility of exercising a totalitarianism, whether visual or in terms of taste (or distaste). Something which, besides, secures one of the threads which we are always encountering when we deal with modern times: *antinomy*.

To be "modern" is "simultaneously revolutionary and conservative: open to new possibilities of experience and adventure, terrorized by the nihilist abyss which so many modern adventures lead to, expecting to create and conserve something real, even when everything around is breaking up. One would say that to be totally modern it is necessary to be anti-modern"[21]. Marshall Bermann puts his finger on the spot. In fact, we live a reality which insistently searches for a breaking with the past, but which has still not found the future, which intends to abolish the model, but has not yet found a new model.

Translated by *David Alan Prescott*

[1] De Quincy, Quatremère, *Considérations Morales sur la Destination Des Ouvrages de L'Art*, Paris, Fayard 1989, p. 9.

[2] De Quincy, Quatremère, *op. cit.*, p. 37.

[3] Stafford, Barbara Maria, *Body Criticism — Imaging the Unseen in Enlightenment Art and Medicine*, Massachusetts, The MIT Press 1993, p. 468.

[4] Cfr. Foucault, Michel, *As Palavras e as Coisas*, Lisbon, Edições 70, 1988, p. 65.

[5] Cfr. Burger, Peter, *Teoria de La Vanguardia*, Barcelona, Península, 1987 and an interview by the author to Isabelle Graw, *Flash Art*, Milan, January/February 1989.

[6] Stafford, Barbara Maria, *op. cit.*, p. 472.

[7] Benjamin, Walter, *Le Concept de Critique Esthétique dans le Romantisme Allemand*, Paris, Flammarion, 1986, p. 113.

[8] Pereira, Miguel Baptista, *Modernidade e Tempo*, Coimbra, Minerva, 1990, p. 52.

[9] Adorno, Theodor W., *Teoria Estética*, Lisbon, Edições 70, 1982, p. 220.

[10] Cfr. Duve, Thierry, *Au Nom de L'Art*, Paris, Minuit, 1989.

[11] Cfr. Foucault, Michel, *As Palavras e as Coisas*, Lisbon, Edições 70, 1988, chap. I.

[12] Duve, *op. cit.*, p. 10.

[13] *Idem*, p. 18.

[14] *Idem*, p. 11.

[15] *Idem*, p. 15.

[16] *Idem*, p. 36.

[17] Cfr. Lyotard, Jean-François, *Dérives à partir de Marx et Freud*, Paris, Bourgois, 1973 (trans. Eng, Drift Works, New York, Semiotext, 1984, pp. 16-17.

[18] Foucault, *op. cit.*, p. 65.

[19] With respect to this point cfr. Carrol, David, *Paraesthetics*, New York-London, Methuen, 1987, p. 31.

[20] Stafford, Barbara Maria, *op. cit.*, p. 472

[21] Bermann, Marshall, *Tudo o que é sólido se dissolve no ar* (Trad. Ana Telo), Lisbon, Edições 70, 1989, p. 13.

THE DISSOLUTION OF FUTURE

José Jiménez

We have become paralysed by a type of mirage. Since its very beginning, the idea of Modernity has been linked with the *fulfilment of a project in time*. But this project — a free and fair society, the predominance of rationality — has gradually spread but never come to fruition, like a promise never kept.

Now we live without a future and without confidence in the fulfilment of the project which has lost its way and for which there is no alternative. The threshold of a new century and an unknown millennium engenders the feeling that everything has reached its end in the *human account of time*.

Actually, this vertigo ignores the fact that the 21st century has already begun, even though the way we count the years says differently. The 20th century ended in 1989, when the Berlin Wall was demolished and the process began which was eventually to lead to the disappearance of the Soviet Union. A new turn in the rootless and convulsed process of modern experience.

The opacity of an obscure age imbues our souls in a world shaped by the techniques and hyper-abundance of communication. Within this particular perspective, open to the unknown, where exactly is art...?

Since the last century, art has been dragging around the eternal question of its death, its final end. And since time dimension is one of its central components, the vertigo of these rapidly passing years, apparently moving in no particular direction, strengthens the feeling of stagnation and loss — the very image of its final and irrevocable disappearance.

1. LIFE IS RAPID, ART IS SLOW

To stop time and capture the moment of fullness. This is a function we have attributed to art for centuries. Speaking of painting and in the age in which the process began to crystallise "art" as an institution (the system of Fine Arts), Leone Battista Alberti stated "it bears within itself a force so divine that painting, as they say about friendship, not only brings the absent into our presence, but it also presents as living those who died centuries ago" (1433: 11).

In Leonardo da Vinci's famous *Parangón*, the superiority of painting over poetry and music has as one of its reasons the fact that the object of the latter two arts is hearing, which Leonardo considers a "less worthy" sense than sight, "since it dies as it is born, and is as impetuous in its birth as in its death" (Da Vinci, 1651: 58). It is the *intensification of the time process* that gives painting its greater worth. While hearing, Leonardo writes, "transmits to the sensibilities the depiction of named things with greater confusion and delay", sight on the other hand "communicates with maximum speed and truth the true figure of what appears before it" (Da Vinci, 1651: 57).

The decisive features, then, are *precision and speed*, which the eye projects onto the pictorial world around it: "Painting presents in an instant the essence of its object to the visual faculty" (Da Vinci, 1651: 57). "In an instant": Leonardo's expression associates within its metaphorical range, this aspect of painting with the speedy lightning flash of time.

For this reason, the harmony of human beauty, in the presence of which the senses tremble, is only lastingly captured in the mirror of painting. "Time", says Leonardo, "destroys in a few years the beauty of such harmony, which does not occur with that same beauty if the painter imitates it, since it conserves it for a long time" (Da Vinci, 1651: 58).

Alberti and Leonardo developed their arguments during the period in which art was separating and differentiating itself from technique. In Leonardo's text, we also notice a confrontation or split between the senses, which is important in the process by which the autonomy of expression of the different arts took shape.

Three centuries later, Lessing's *Laocoonte* (1766) gives us a fully defined theoretical formulation of this autonomy of expression of each of the arts. Although his purpose is the opposite of Leonardo's — to highlight the superiority of poetry over painting — Lessing also associates the specificity of visual art with mimesis or representation of the moment.

According to Lessing, the very object of "painting" (visual art) is spatial representation and the imitation of bodies, rather different from "poetry" (literature), which imitates action and is therefore a temporal art. However, Lessing (1766: 106) concedes that "all bodies exist not only in space, but also in time. They have duration, and at any time of this duration they may display a different aspect or enter into different relations with other things".

Lessing's conclusion is that, due to the foregoing, painting may also imitate action, if only in an allusive way; i.e., *by means of bodies*. But, taking Lessing's text to its logical extreme, what it implies is that visual art allows for the *corporeal representation of time*. Lessing considers this to be a limitation: painting can only use a single element of the action, and this constitutes in reality the ultimate reason for its links with the representation of a time of fullness, *with the moment*, as Leonardo had already noted.

Visual art does not operate through the serialisation of its signs. It is thus forced to choose from among the different moments "the most pregnant of all, the one which allows one to take fullest advantage of both the preceding and ensuing ones" (Lessing, 1766: 107).

To stop time and to give (figurative) embodiment to the moment — and not just to any moment, but rather to the *most intense* moment. What art permits is no less than a rupture in the time sequence, a stopping of the unrepeatable flow of time. Naturally, this mission performed by art shows us the profound link between its destiny and the process of modern culture.

The very idea of modernity "could only be conceived in the tangle of an awareness of specific time, i.e., that of *historical time*, linear and irreversible, irresistibly moving forward" (Calinescu, 1987: 23). In fact, our traditional conception of art, the one which, with very few changes, is still in force today, began to take shape (as I have already mentioned) at this time, which perceived itself as "different" from the immediately preceding centuries — the age which lived its present as a "Renaissance" of Graeco-Roman antiquity and distanced itself from the immediate past by inventing the obscure label of "Middle Ages".

And yet, it was during these mediaeval centuries that the perception of time as an unrepeatable flow spread, based on the eschatological doctrines of Christianity. However, when the space of representation, of mimesis, was no longer subordinated to religious beliefs, and when, in addition to thematic autonomy, art also gained independence with regard to technique, it was to become one of the few possible forms of stopping the linear flow and of appropriating the fleeing moment. To be modern meant to live linear time and at the same time to represent it (sequentially or corporeally) in the arts.

The decline of organised religion and the intense secularisation of all dimensions of public life implicit in the development of modern culture leaves the human being completely alone in the presence of this fleeing time, which pierces like an arrow. The best symbolic profile of this experience of *time as anguish* which characterises modernity is Goethe's Faust.

Faust lives eternal youth not as an end in itself, but rather as a way to experience life intensely, drunk as he is with the idea of action. He thinks he has wasted his life with books and his quest for further knowledge. His haughty bet with Mephistopheles implies the illusion that he is able to deceive the lightning strike of time and he does not even desire to stop the moment. This is how the bet is made: "If I ever say to a single moment: Stop, you are so beautifull / you can tie me up with chains" (Goethe, 1808: 50).

Obsessed with action and focusing on his impulse to dominate the world by technical means, Faust, at the end of the day a modern man like all of us, ends up trying to hold the moment, thus losing his bet: "I would like to say at this moment: / Stop, you are so beautiful! / The traces of my days on earth / Cannot be eternally dissipated…" (Goethe, 1831: 339). Note that the moment which Faust wishes to hold is the *aesthetic* moment, the time of fullness in which we live the experience of beauty.

That is the privileged horizon of art — this unrepeatable, intense experience, which makes us forget that we are essentially transitory and fleeting, and which allows us to live, if only for a moment, the moment of aesthetic fullness, *outside time*, beyond its implacable march.

Only the various forms of *ecstasy*: mystical, amorous, hallucinatory, can be considered to equal art's capacity to make us live this fullness of the moment. In this ecstasy the notion of succession also breaks or evaporates, due to this stunning blow which plunges us into an experience with no before or after and which we would love to hold *for ever*.

Now this mystical ecstasy is extremely difficult to attain, much more so in an age in which Western culture sees its future marked by the public decline of religion. Hallucinatory ecstasy outside the ritual contexts which place it under control becomes destructive and annihilating, as can be seen nowadays in its secular version of widespread drug consumption. Finally, amorous ecstasy, which springs up in life itself, *fades* just as quickly.

Only art makes our eyes shine with the illusion of something lasting, of *something which remains*. And in the development of our cultural tradition, we deposit in it a *rising* rhythm, an inspiration which has its source in sensitivity and attains the flight of the spirit. A promise not only of happiness (Stendhal) but of *temporal fullness*. Therefore, in the presence of the fleeting turmoil of life, art, within this tradition, *moves slowly*. As the Swiss artist Heinrich Füssli wrote at the end of the 18th century, "Life is rapid, art is slow".

2. THE FEELING OF MOVEMENT MADE ETERNAL

Art slow…? If tradition situated artistic work beyond the fleeing rapidity of life, the appearance of the avant-garde proclaimed a new approximation of art to life, the abandonment of academies and, in general terms, the condemnation of the past. The stress on dynamism, speed, even haste, have come to characterise the art of our century.

In 1910, in the *Manifesto of Futurist Painters*, written by Umberto Boccioni, it is said that while the Ancients sought inspiration in the religious sphere, "we ought to seek it in the tangible prodigies of modern life, in the iron network of speed that covers the earth, in transatlantic liners, in Dreadnoughts, in the marvellous aircraft which plough the skies, in the tremendous audacity of underwater navigators, in the spasmodic struggle for the conquest of the unknown".

What best defines the new situation is the expression "spasmodic struggle" — *combat* and *convulsion*. To situate oneself in the avant-garde was, in effect, to assume the *moral responsibility* of art. To sustain the belief that an innovative artistic "language" would open the way at the front line to the progress of the whole of humanity. But the spasmodic character of this struggle did not appear only as a result of this combative attitude. It also had to do with the extreme, intense assumption in the art of the spirit (focused on action and the future, turned towards "progress") of modernity. Rimbaud's slogan "It is necessary to be absolutely modern" had opened a new horizon in which artistic activity was conceived under the sign of a distancing from tradition.

This initial moment of the exaltation of the "radiant" image of the future, with all its ingenuousness and that militarism which causes us so much concern nowadays, is, in my opinion, what best defines the unsure, labyrinthine terrain into which art was adventuring.

In another manifesto published the same year, *Futurist Painting*, also written by Boccioni, we read, "For us, the gesture is not a *stopped moment* of universal dynamism: it is also the *feeling of movement* made eternal as such". This is a reiteration (in and from art!) of the wager with Mephistopheles. "We", futurist artists and artists of the future are not going to stop the moment, but rather make "eternal" the dynamism of action. The Faustian spirit and the will to dominate the world enters and spreads like poison in artistic networks. And of course, once again, the wager *will be lost*.

"Everything moves, everything runs and everything gathers speed", the futurists said, and years later, Le Corbusier stated "The youth of today has an engine in its stomach and an aircraft in its heart".

On the one hand, as Georg Simmel has already indicated (1903), the immanent process of modern culture had led, by the shape and form of large cities, to an acute and nervous intensification of the *tempo* of life. On the other hand, the development of technology had made the traditional pre-eminence of art over technology an extremely problematic question.

The process of schism between art and life, which began in 15th-century Italy, implied making art into an essential model and hierarchical reference point for all artisan practices. This was something which was still valid in the Romantic period and which was pointed out with perspicacity by Novalis (1798-1799: 358): "The artist directs artisan practices. By means of a higher unity he concentrates various crafts which acquire greater significance due to this higher concentration".

But as the 19th century advanced, the development of industrialisation led to the progressive obsolescence of artisan manufacture, and the emancipation of technology from manual labour was also to lead to its dependence on art. The "good hand" and the bodily eye of the artist no longer served as a reference in a world which was increasingly shaped by the machine and represented by the "mechanical eye". This convulsion was the inspiration behind the appearance of the avant--garde, and which led to the new relationship which the avant-garde attempted to establish with technology.

The *break with mimesis* — classic representation (with its different registers in the various arts) — is inseparable from this complex process, and in the specific case of the visual arts, inseparable from the impact made by the invention of photography — visual reproduction using a machine.

On 21 May 1853, Eugène Delacroix made a note in his Diary of one of the greatest instances of this impact. Together with his friends, he carried out an experiment which he had already performed alone two days previously: they compared some engravings with a series of not particularly high quality photographic nudes. According to Delacroix, the result was "a feeling of aversion, almost of disgust" for the engravings. This together with a two-edged conclusion: "Truly, if a man of genius were to use the Daguerreotype as it should be used, he will rise to unthought of heights". This is an acknowledgement of the aesthetic *expressive potential* of the new medium. But Delacroix also observed: "Until now, this machine art has provided only a detestable service: it means that we lose masterpieces, yet does not satisfy us completely".

This is one of the earliest and most sincere admissions of the *profound questioning of the traditional, manual system of artistic representation* brought about by the new "machine art".

Photography made it possible to fix a corporeal image of time, to stop the moment visually, without depending on the privileged hand of the artist. Everyone could gain access to this simply by means of the camera. The mechanical eye records everything: loved ones, happy moments... It also brings with it new areas of vision: the nudity of the body exposed to pornographic view, the naked representation of death (there are few images as impressive as those of the dead of the Paris Commune in their coffins), or the perception of the human masses as a single unit. Put to the service of political power, as documentary support, photography soon became one of the most effective methods of social control.

All of them are interventions in the flow of time which, however, due to the fact that they may be reproduced and are available in seemingly infinite numbers, end up producing an even more intense experience of the fleetingness of the moment. Classical art spiritualised the moment, made it transcendent, "beautiful" or "graceful". It transmitted the experience and the promise of a time of fullness. The mechanical reproduction of the image provides the levelling of any moment, the fixing of the anonymous instant and, in the final analysis, *the indifferentiation of time*.

All moments are superimposed on each other in obscurity, and time, the future we thought we controlled, becomes even more densely opaque. Let us remember the verses of Paul Celan: "INSTANTS, of whom we're signs / No light sleeps / Non-beings from everywhere / gather yourself / and (standing) you must remain". (1968: 11)

3. FROZEN IMAGE, REVERSIBLE IMAGE

To remain standing, in spite of the chaos into which they had been plunged, was the drive which moved the inter-war avant-garde. A combative moral position, rooted in the melting down of the old society and the labour pains of a new world. Never in modern times had art attained a higher degree of politicisation. This, in fact, led to a more acute intensification of its developmental linearity, its temporal determination as "progress".

The artistic scene retained the form of an ascending line, like an evolutionary process. Any tendency towards codification was condemned as sterile repetition. If emancipation from technique was tending to make our world a kingdom of *redundancy*, art laid its claims on the language of surprise and the sign of the unrepeatable. Innovation and rupture have in fact been the central axes of art in our century.

But the moral and mould-breaking impulse of the avant-garde has been weakening for some time now. When it is "the new" that becomes tradition (Harold Rosenberg), art ends up being reduced to a gesture and remaining content with that, it ends up emptying itself in stereotype.

I think that the most important stage in this change took place at the time when the first mass societies began to take shape. This, in inter-war Europe, was at an incipient stage: a mass communication cultural system, articulated into a cohesive whole, was now definitively becoming consolidated in the Anglo-Saxon world, especially in the USA, after the end of the war.

Pop art is the most intense instance of this consolidation, in which a new world of images is born. Formalist research or committed/engaged and mould-breaking themes are substituted by the reproduction in art of forms of communication and the expressive procedures of the new culture. There is thus a large degree of inter-meshing between mass communication media, advertising, industrial design and art.

Roy Lichtenstein substituted painting with the vignette of the comic. As an advertiser, Andy Warhol turned the spotlight on the now famous (in artistic as well as consumer terms) can of soup. The world of artistic representation, impregnated since its inception during the Renaissance with a sacred halo, had now become definitively and irreversibly *secular*. In addition, the avant-garde dream of a new world was substituted by the certainty of the mirror and Art had stopped putting forward alternatives. This is why nowadays, critical attention has once again begun to reconsider the importance of pop art with more interest than ever, since it anticipated all of the perplexities and disillusion of these *fin-de-siècle* years.

In the sudden "secularisation" of art brought about by the pop art vision (which seen today in perspective and in comparison with the historic avant-garde may turn out to seem almost brutal) we may once more identify a feature specifically linked to the modern process. I am referring to the tendency towards "secularisation" and disenchantment with the world, according to Max Weber's expression.

But if we wish to go even further into the situation art is experiencing in this new fin-de-siècle it is necessary to be aware, above all of how far the schism with the technical *has disappeared*, or is in the process of disappearing. Besides, in a world where the technical has impregnated communication, and communication has found its way to the very centre of art, the old hierarchy has now *been inverted*: the technical has become the ideal model, a point of reference for art.

Mechanical reproduction has now invaded creative work and displaced the former importance of the manual. The formal and technical aspects of visual art are today basically the same as those of the mass media and advertising.

Now we know that the new Mephistopheles with whom avant-garde art could only lose its bet has no demonic or human features, but rather mechanical and technical characteristics. I am not speaking in a Mannichean sense: in no case is it possible to identify technology with "evil" in the ethical sense.

It irreversible spread and the expansion of its predominance has produced a *new feeling of time*, generated to a large extent by the widespread use of images. This is an *anthropological* and cultural dimension, which does not only affect art. It also has to do with the collapse of projects of total emancipation, conceived on the basis of linear time.

The process of technical reproduction of images (of all, not only visual, images) allows for their mass production and reception. But this way, art empties itself of meaning and the various communicative techniques appropriate its procedures and findings, aestheticising life and stylising existence.

We must speak not only of fleetingness and speed, or the vertiginous succession of images which come and go. It was into this point that the densest operation of pop art entered: the individualisation of images from mass culture and their becoming fixed, which redeems them from the voracious flow of time.

Even more important is the double possibility in the use of the image, which is increasingly possible in mass culture: the fact that they may be *frozen* and are *reversible*. This is already an everyday experience. We may stop and thus appropriate any image. It is also possible to reverse its flow, to make it move forwards or backwards.

We have therefore moved beyond what was possible with photography: we may not only stop time but also break its sequence. The cultural perception of time is dissolved in *fragmentation*, a new *porosity*. The times have become more obscure and are even more confusing, they are superimposed on each other and interpenetrative.

What we are actually living is a dissolution of the future (*There's no Future*), in which time has a *cyclical*, *circular* profile. The ascending line, the arrow of time has been diluted. In this world, the counterpoising of the avant-garde against tradition disappears and art's pretension to autonomy is now out of bounds.

It is this possibility of freezing the image, already existing within our culture for a century, that leads to both the accentuation of *Narcissism* and the *pornographic* impregnation implicit in our contemporary gaze. This is a diffuse and all-englobing impregnation and produces a specific form of emptying art of meaning: *kitsch*, which so widespread these days.

But the frozen yet reversible image also puts the artist on a path of *experimentation* with the crossing of languages and techniques, and within a process of *appropriation of the body* cut and fragmented by the massive use of images.

The first aspect presupposes research into forms of expression, a new line for the emancipation of art with regard to technique, but using and appropriating its supports. To liberate forms and procedures from a merely communicative use, to break and blend the various languages of information allows art to *distance itself* within the space of representation.

The second aspect, which assumes the loss of the whole idea of the unity of mimesis, proclaims the will for the unrepeatable and underlines besieged individuality faced by the anonymity of indifferentiation and the electronic mutilation of bodies.

In order for art to continue to exist as such, it must make us capable of participating in an experience of *temporal fullness*, in an age in which this fullness can no longer project itself forward towards the future but can only exist as a redemption of the *moment of beauty* in the undifferentiated circle of time in which we live.

It seems to me that this is the new cross-roads at which art stands at this fin-de-siècle — no longer avant-garde or tradition, but a formal and thematic *compromise* with a new temporal sensibility, with a creative (and therefore critical) use of images. Or even *disappearance* into technique, blending into that technical-communicative unity which constitutes the hyper-aestheticised languages of mass culture. What we are seeing is the necessary birth of a *new moral* of artistic activity or its *dissolution*.

Translated by *Nigel Thomas*

BIBLIOGRAPHICAL REFERENCES

ALBERTI, L. B.

(1435) *Sobre la pintura*, spanish edition by J. Dols, Fernando Torres editor, Valencia, 1975

CALINESCU, M.

(1987) *Cinco caras de la modernidad*, spanish translation by M. T. Beguiristain, Tecnos, Madrid, 1991

CELAN, P.

(1968) *Hebras de Sol*, bilingual edition, spanish translation by M. Fernández-Palacios and J. Siles, Visor, Madrid, 1990

DA VINCI, L.

(1651) *Tratado de la pintura*, A. González García (ed.), Editora Nacional, Madrid, 1979

DELACROIX, E.

El Puente de la visión. Anthology from Diarios, introduction and notes by G. Solana, spanish translation by M. D. Díaz Vaillagou, Tecnos, Madrid, 1987

GOETHE, J. W.

(1808 e 1831) *Fausto*, Parts I and II, introduction by F. Palau, spanish translation and notes by J. M. Valverde, Planeta, Barcelona, 1980

LESSING, G. E.

(1766) *Laocoonte*, introduction and spanish translation by E. Barjau, Tecnos, Madrid, 1990

NOVALIS

(1798-1799) *La enciclopedia*, spanish translation by F. Montes of volume I of *Fragmentos*, Fundamentos, Madrid, 1976

SIMMEL, G.

(1903) «Las grandes urbes y la vida del espíritu», *El individuo y la libertad. Ensayos de crítica de la cultura*, spanish translation and prologue by S. Mas, Península, Barcelona, 1986.

AUGUSTO ALVES DA SILVA

Born 1963, Lisbon
Lives and works in Lisbon

PHOTOMATON AND COMMON SENSE

Our first reaction when faced with these photographs might be to try to identify the people, the places and perhaps to consider that someone we know is there. Besides, it seems that there is nothing else to see or to admire. On the contrary, everything seems to be very boring. The people aren't laughing, aren't crying, aren't showing anything. They themselves seem bored. Only one child is distracted by a toy. It is the exception which confirms the rule. And the worst thing is that we end up understanding that we don't know them from "anywhere". So why look at these photographs? Why take these photographs?

Has the photographer tricked us? Are these photographs of "flesh and blood" people, or mere registers of wax models by the Gévin Museum or Madame Tussaud's? There is no one famous here. The number of people who will recognise someone, besides the people themselves feeding up their self-satisfaction, besides relatives and friends, is zero. But, not even those will be charmed. At home, doing what? Are these special occasions? Judging by the tables and the spreads laid out they are certainly not. There are no birthday cakes, no special dinner services. So why these photographs?

Let us try a more "lyrical" approach: light usually provides a good pretext for some common metaphors. Light fills space equally and discreetly surrounds the objects and the bodies. The interiors photographed have their story and the pictorial reference could be Vermeer. Or, in this case, because of the austerity of those portrayed, by the manner in which they are looking at the spectator-photographer, some contemporary Holbein. Despite the change of settings — all of the rooms are different — there are no great shades, nor violent contrasts, which might distinguish them from each other. Yet all the photographs have their lamps, but none of them seem to be turned on (or the light from them doesn't produce a visible effect). And the windows one sees in three of them are closed. We may state with some certainty that the other spaces also have closed windows. Even the doors are closed. The light is neither interior nor exterior. Therefore, the treatment of the light, something so convulsive and traditional in the photographic image, appears insipient and very unseductive.

Where does the light come from anyway? If it is not from the windows, nor the lamps, nor from the outside nor inside, where does it come from? These photographs were taken *against* the natural light, most certainly, but they were also taken *against* artificial light. Only one possibility comes to my mind: this is "photographical" light par excellence, the light with which one makes copies of documents — books, manuscripts, drawings, ID cards, birth and death certificates, property registers, etc. — or advertising products — detergents, jewels, cars, etc… A more or less neutral light which allows the bodies to become free from the floor, releasing themselves from the shadows projected. The world that these photographs represent, if they represent anything, is a world without days, without nights — a flat two-dimensional, bureaucratic world. Through light one reaches no less a sordid place.

Perhaps, then, one should take recourse in a more logical observation, supposedly more objective and factual. The photographs are shown as a group and were produced according to a precise leitmotiv: the family. Are there really relations of kinship between these people, detectable by physical analogies? It is probable. We look for these similarities, these resemblances, and we always end up discovering something. It is a recourse of protocol involving liking and appreciation, or, also, of beginning or continuing a conversation "just to fill it out"; often, only to show visual perspicacity. Isn't this what happens when someone takes pleasure in finding traces of the father or the mother in the child, even when the latter is still a wet new-born babe?

The structural habits of relationship revealed by a possible hierarchy of positions relative to the photographical setting up is also not satisfied. The characters blur into one another. Even when they are repeated, that is, when they appear in more than one photograph, they don't alter their posture or their attitude. The idea of the family, hypothetically presented here by the sequential form, reveals no temporality. Or rather, it cancels out the very idea of a sequence, and remains a group of images. Is this a family just because they are sitting together around tables, which happen to be always round? What data do we have for their interpretation? Does Augusto Alves da Silva have something against the family?

The family, for many people the basis for a supposed primordial order, is here put into confrontation with the haphazard nature of those portrayed. There is no protagonist, no star, who might become a pattern. To shuffle and begin again, seems to be the final end reserved for these photographs. It is the supposed family order versus the equally supposed photographical order. But the results, as one may see, are imprecise. There is nothing verifiable despite the photogenic characteristics of these photographs — light, colours, figures, positions, compositions, settings — they indicate everything in the sense of and in the desire of evidence. But are the evidences obligatorily aseptic? Things are evidences when they do not show what they mean or what they are, and when they start showing *only* what they show and denounce their way of showing it. Is it the promiscuity of these photographs that is, after all, the only tangible proof of anthropological promiscuity?

If we wish to exaggerate, Augusto Alves da Silva makes photocopies, not photographs. His secret desire, if he could, would be to use a portable colour photocopier. I think that his photographs — or photocopies — are as funny as they are political. They are images in which one looks for committed commentary and testimony, accompanied by a joke, like those that we only understand half an hour later, without realising it. The politics of the image, just like its humour, necessarily have to do with the denunciation of the illusory neutrality of the photograph, with illusions of the neutral light and colours and with its iconical character. In Augusto Alves da Silva's photographs, things "seem to be what they are" and "to be what they seem" is always at play until a possible diluting. It is this ambition to *photomaton* which runs throughout his works. From an essay on the Algarve in 1988/89 until the work recently finished on the Instituto Superior Técnico (Higher Technical Institute), going through *Algés-Trafaria, 1990* (1990) and *A Cidade dos Objectos* (*The City of Objects*) (1991), it is the contexts of photographical communication which are being explored.

In the field of photography in Portugal, his images are against the light and dandyish, bent over, contrasted and dark photographs. These are upright, balanced and clear, to the point of going unnoticed, of not showing anything "special", of being commonplace. But there is something in which Augusto Alves da Silva is mistaken. His images, in wishing to be against beauty, against any form of emotional enticement, and giving absolute priority to their descriptive aspects, to the extent of questioning them in such a radical manner, are condemned, no matter how paradoxical it may seem, to seduction. What seems to me to be profoundly present in his photographs is this exploration of photography as a perfect example of 20th Century *sensus communis*. And today there are few more dangerous and more deeply seductive things than *sensus communis*.

Translated by *David Alan Prescott*

António Sena

Augusto Alves da Silva
Such a nice family, 1992
Series of six photographs
Fujichrome
75 x 93 cm each

GERARDO BURMESTER

Born 1953, Oporto
Lives and works in Oporto

GERARDO BURMESTER: ATELIER (1994)
ON SCEPTICISM AS AN EXERCISE IN SEDUCTION

DOUBT[1]

EVERYTHING THAT ANYONE MAY SAY ABOUT
WHAT THEY DO MAKES IT RELATIVE[2]

Gerardo Burmester's recent work starts from the assumption of a relative scepticism, rooted in the dilemmas equated within it on the condition of art, space and materials used, or questions like those of authorship and what is well done. This scepticism becomes an exercise in suspicion, when the artist hands over his projects to artifices which carry them out in a perfectionist manner, in an ironical exercise which turns them into strange, singular objects, prototypes for others which will no longer be produced based on them. Doubt is raised when one uses wood, leather and felt intersected in luxuriously finished-off exercises of combination, within an exercise of derision where the drawing is contaminated by the virtuality of a deceptive, non-functional, design, but without the arrogance of the aestheticised object.

In a recent piece like *Sobre o Desenho* (*On Drawing*) (1994), wood and felt form the lexicon of a strange grammar. A grammar whose aim is not the exercise of a language, but the suspicion of a language. It is a false sculpture where the object appears as a derision of the drawing. The materials are only part of a game of space, within the choreographical tension established between them. The design becomes an irony consequent from the drawing and this is questioned in the context of its functional or decorative contaminations. The relationship between design and sculpture is equally subverted in this piece, whose craft-like dimensions is singularized by its inability to be reproduced in a critical horizon of post-industrial reception. The three dimensionality is presented as a state of resistence to the status of drawing or sculpture, just like when, in another context, Donald Judd proclaimed the use of the three dimensions as an obvious alternative: "It opens to everything. Many of the reasons for this use are negative, points against painting and sculpture, and since both are common sources, the negative reasons are common-age"[3].

— NOTHING HERE IS REAL — JUST A WAY OF PASSING THE TIME[4]

From suspicion about making art and what the grammar of its elements supply us with, to the exercising of doubt on space and the very conditions of the viewer's visibility, there is *Amarelos--Arquipélagos-Vermelhos* (*Red Yellow Archipelagoes*) (1992), an installation which Gerardo Burmester presented in the Oporto City Customs House. An artificial landscape divided by two colours prompted by geometrical puzzles made of stainless steel boxes, some red, some yellow, in which sideless bridges, wooden and felt boxes, and satin objects rest, or rather float and are reflected on a terrain of wood and paving-stone contrasting with the irridescence of this divided and excessive landscape which the viewer can only look at but not cross, as if it were a mirage. The viewer experiences nothing more than an illusion, that of the conversion of space in time, which is intensified by percussion music and Gregorian chant. The ostentatious reduction of the visitor to a spectator conditions his own capacity to see, turning the space established into the rhetorical redundance of a false virtual reality. The objects presented within it are removed from reality, reduced to their condition of things which reveal no more than the magical appearance of not being there. Their secret is maximum visibility, the labyrinth of reflections which multiplies them, aware of the seduction arising from the knowledge that *there is no "heart" of things. These things are only surface and nothing more*[5].

We are far from the Utopia that John Cage announced when he proposed the intersection between art and experience, considering that *Art comes from a form of experimental condition in which experiments are done with life*[6].

In this case the work of the artist with space subverts the dynamics of the process of installation in its pro-positive and/or Utopian virtualities, making it instead a non-space, an atopia where seeing too much becomes a state of deconstruction of any possibility of feeling or experience.

CONTAMINATIONS[7]

THE SUBJECT MATTER OF CREATION IS CHAOS[8]

The whole creative process may be converted into its impure dimension as a contamination, understood in the matrical sense that Barnett Newman gave to the word *Chaos*, when he described the work of the artist as "engaged in a true act of discovery in the creation of new forms and symbols that will have the living quality of creation"[9]. Chaos, just as doubt, is exercised here as a methodological process of contamination between ideas, forms and materials aimed at in the pieces by Burmester with the titles *Percurso (Route)* (1993) and *Sal, Vapor, Vidro, Madeira e Feltro (Salt, Steam, Glass, Wood and Felt)* (1993). In *Percurso*, a felt carpet rolled out from a wooden cylinder extends into another similar carpet made of rock salt. The impure whites of the felt and the rock salt complete each other within a process of reciprocal corrosion contrasted by the perfection and clarity of the wooden piece from which they appear to have come. There is a latent violence in this piece, as well as a strange calm, both reinforced by the paradoxically paralysed movement from which it flows. It would be possible to describe the tension between the materials by using a rhetorical figure, oxymoron. In language, oxymoron means the contradiction between neighbouring words which are morphologically different, such as a noun and and adjective (a classic example in relation to a rhetorical description of *Percurso*: "obscure clarity"). The complementary nature between the salt and the felt is nothing more than an illusion here, and the violence of this illusion resides in the difference which connects and separates the two matters, which mixes them, or rather, which contaminates them. If this process of contamination could be described by an everyday dictionary as a

contagion; infection; corruption; stain; impurity; deposit of a radioactive substance in a potentially dangerous place, or at least an undesirable one (Lat. Contaminatione)[10].

the threat contained in these stretchings of meanings is made more physically material in a work like *Sal, Vapor, Vidro, Madeira e Feltro* by means of the process of evaporation of the salt deposited in a glass box, which is carried out by two vaporizers. Above the glass, another, larger box (wood lined with felt) provides the whole piece with the dimension of a threatened solidity. The fact that the artist entitles this with the names of the materials is not innocent. The enumeration deconstructs the illusion of any metaphorical reading which the work might give rise to. The process of contamination here expressed by this mechanics of fluids in which there is evaporation is made more dense by the heightening of the proximity between the salt, the glass and the felt, made lighter by the action of the steam which impregnates them and insinuates itself within them. The whole results from a dynamic process of "contagion" or "corruption" arising from "stains, impurities", that is new forms coming from a physical process which alters the work of art independently of the decisions of the creator or the viewer, being surprised by the new configurations that some of the elements weave amongst themselves within a process of recognition of that "living quality of creation" mentioned by Newman to describe the demiurge of a chaos which is the origin of all works of art. Unlike Newman, however, there is no demiurgical intention in Gerardo Burmester. Art becomes a process of dynamic relation between the elements that form it, just like any other natural or artificial physical process, independent of the dominion of its consequences on the part of the creator. Burmester's relative scepticism is here clearly far from the power inherent to the cosmogony of this chaos accepted by Newman, and is clearly critical of any demiurgical intentions by the author of the work of art.

As the artist himself confesses, *there is a great effort in contradicting that which, for me, is identified with stability. Perhaps only disorder is really creative and only a non-definitive creation is really worthwhile after all*[11].

An example and a summary of this "non-definitive creation" is doubtlessly Burmester's latest piece, *Atelier* (1994), presented in the exhibition this catalogue describes:

ATELIER
CELA VAUT LA PEINE D'Y PASSER UNE NUIT

In 1920, Max Ernst produces a small work, *The Master's Bedroom*, in which, using a technique of frottage, he goes over a previously painted gouache work which depicts an empty room, and lays a series of transfers from a children's catalogue. One can read a sentence, in German and in French: "la chambre à coucher de Max Ernst cela vaut la peine d'y passer une nuit"[12].

In 1994, Gerardo Burmester presents *Atelier*, a piece formed of a room with wooden walls, floor and ceiling, lined inside with a square of impermeable white cloth. A slight entrance allows the viewer's visit yet makes it difficult. Inside, vaporizers make the atmosphere dense, hot and humid. On the floor several objects, rolls and piles of drawings on felt among other things, are spread out in irregular geometry, as if they have been scattered by unfathomable chance.

IMITATION OF CHANCE IS NOT PERFECT (IT IS USELESS TO STRESS THIS)[13]

Between these two works by Max Ernst and Burmester one should not overdo the comparisons. However, the objects' relationship with the space in Burmester represents, in its de-realization, a process of evolving of which Ernst was in some way a forerunner, in the apparently casual drawing of his compositional process. The figure of the room, an interior space of refuge in time and in imagination, is present in both works. Ernst's blind walls are lined with white in Burmester. In Ernst, the figures obtained through the transfers (a suspended window crossed by a tree, a bed, a table, several animals of various sizes-bear, sheep, whale, bat, fish and snake) are open to the construction of meaning in their ingenuous and perverse association, like the relation of a polymorphic sexuality, indecisive as to its interiority and its exteriorization. In Burmester, the outer image of the object appears almost like a wooden house, perfectionistically finished off, the image of cold, hardly accessible luxury. Inside, the space of the house is occupied by the place of the bedroom as an announcer of a virtual intimacy available to the eye of the viewer, but protected from him by the sensorial experience of the heat and the humidity. The white-lined inside, like the humid and thermal density, do not make this experience a means of apprehending and penetrating within the artist's space, and instead appear as a barrier, a particular effect of strangeness. The visitor is endowed with an intrusive gaze within a context that is strange to him and even hostile. If the figure of the bedroom holds all the possible connotations of intimacy and sexuality, it is endowed here with the allegory of the creative process, establishing with it a relationship of distancing, fragmented by the inventory of residues and sensations which it contains.

The inventory creates a curious relationship between *The Master's Bedroom* and *Atelier*: the chance association of figures from a child's imagination in their relationship with the background which defines the possibilities of feeling (Ernst) is succeeded by a loose relationship of objects which are no more than feigned residues of the artist's work with a space without which they would be nothing (Burmester). The process of putting the transfer on the painted paper is substituted by the perceiving of the heat and the humidity which fix the relationship of a set of objects with the place in which they are set to the viewer's gaze. In both cases, the deep relationship with the objects contained within them is a pure relationship of inclusion of singular sets within a wider set.

In *Atelier*, the objects pretend to be rhetorical exercises of simulation of the artist's personal work.

There are no instruments of work as would be normal in a literal interpretation of the title, because the objects create their own legitimacy as a product and as a desire to "see" and not to "do". Designed felts are piled upon each other, here and there. The drawing is however hidden by a process of accumulation which de-sacralizes them as objects of art so that they can be felt as a far-off vestige of a "making of art". Art is only present in this space due to its memory without nostalgia.

One thus accepts the drawing as an operative concept and not a means of expression. Each element installed in the space denies itself as an artistic object. It has no autonomy, and is within a spatial relationship which situates it and indifferentiates it. *Atelier* is a piece which accumulates interrogations on the status of the work of art nowadays, without representing a search for possible answers. The scepticism is felt in the suspension of any certainty or judgement. The creative space is hidden within an intimate cocoon, but exposed because it is travelled and glimpsed at. As if everything had to be confirmed once more. Like when romanticism denied itself on reflexion by stating that "the impression that works of art give us is of a more reflexive nature, and everything that they arouse in us needs ulterior verification"[14].

The space of art turns into the exercise of doubt and of all the principles of certainty. It is, however, or perhaps because of this.

CELA VAUT LA PEINE D'Y PASSER UNE NUIT.

Translated by David Alan Prescott

João Fernandes

[1] Piece by Gerardo Burmester (1993), formed of a felt and a leaning glass, where one may read "DUVIDE" (DOUBT).

[2] Statements by the author in an interview to Eduardo Paz Barroso. "Gerardo Burmester: I've always painted in a constant rupture", in *Jornal de Notícias*, Oporto, 15.1.1988.

[3] Donald Judd in *Arts Yearbook*, 8, NY, 1965, p. 74.

[4] António Franco Alexandre, in *Oasis*, Assírio e Alvim, Lisboa, 1993, p. 22.

[5] "Non esiste un 'cuore' delle cose. Esse sono sol superficie e null'altro". Mario Perniola, in *Enigmi. Il momento egizio nella società e nell'arte*, Edizioni Costa & Nolan, Genova, 1990, p. 54.

[6] "Art comes from a kind of experimental condition in which one experiments with living". Quoted by Germano Celant in *Art Povera*, London, 1969, p. 225.

[7] Title of an exhibition by Gerardo Burmester in 1993 in the Galeria Pedro Oliveira, Oporto.

[8] "The subject matter of creation is chaos". Barnett Newman, in *Selected Writings and Interviews*, UCLA Press, L.A., p. 139.

[9] *Idem.*

[10] *Dicionário da Língua Portuguesa*, Porto Editora, 5th ed.

[11] Statements by the artist to Eduardo Paz Barroso, "Gerardo Burmester: I've always painted within a constant rupture", in *Jornal de Notícias*, Oporto, 15.1.1988.

[12] Ref. in Rosalind Krauss, *The Optical Unconscious*. The MIT Press, Cambridge, Massachussetts, 1993, p. 55.

[13] Carlos de Oliveira, *Finisterra*, Sá da Costa, Lisboa, 1978, p. 90.

[14] Hegel, *Vorlesungen üher die Ästhetik*, Frankfurt am Main, 1983, t. XIII, p. 23.

Gerardo Burmester
Sobre o Desenho, *1994*
Galeria Alda Cortez, Lisbon
Wood and felt
270 x 160 x 80 cm
Photo: Laura Castro Caldas and Paulo Cintra

Gerardo Burmester
Amarelos-Arquipélagos-Vermelhos, *1992*
Caves da Alfândega do Porto — Installation
Jornadas de Arte Contemporânea do Porto
Stainless steel, colour varnish, wood, felt,
satin, earth and gravel
Photo: António Pinto

PEDRO CABRITA REIS

Born 1956, Lisbon
Lives and works in Lisbon

Pedro Cabrita Reis
Os Observadores / Atlas Coelestis VI, *1994*
Glass, mirror, rubber hose, steel vessel with clay,
wood, plastic tube, ironed string and found object
Installation with variable dimensions
Photo: José Pessoa

Pedro Cabrita Reis
Echo Der Welt III, 1994
Mala Galerija, Ljubljana
Wood, foam, glass, juta stripes and ropes, felt,
electric wire, bulbs, copper tubes,
rubber hoses and a found stool
233 x 326 x 152 cm
Constructed between 24th and 27th January 1993,
«in situ», with the collaboration
of France Mlakar and Boris Fister
under the supervision of Nives Zalokar
Artist's collection
Photo: Lado Mlekuz

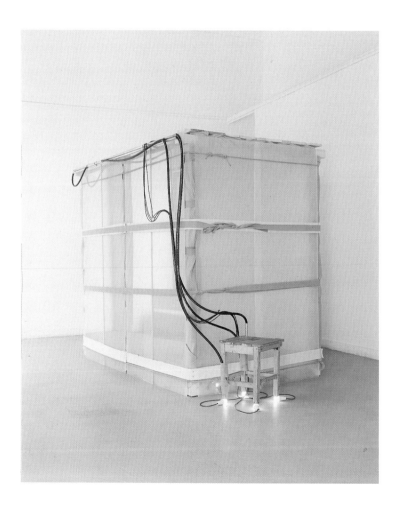

Pedro Cabrita Reis
Sistema de Constelações / Atlas Coelestis IV, 1994,
CAM / FCG, Lisbon
Wood, masonite, flannel, juta, glass, rubber hoses
Variable size
Constructed in May 1994, in CAM / FCG,
under the supervision of Manuel Piçarra
Artist's collection
Photo: Laura Castro Caldas and Paulo Cintra

PEDRO CALAPEZ

Born 1953, Lisbon
Lives and works in Lisbon

D'APRÈS PIRANESI

1. Pedro Calapez has at several stages in his career used the works of historical Western artists as the starting point for various series of his own works. Examples of this have been his reference to Giotto in the series *Pinturas sobre madeira, (Paintings on wood)* shown at the Sociedade Nacional de Belas Artes in 1984, and in some of the drawings on wood exhibited at the Gulbenkian in 1989, as well as to Fra Angelico in the exhibition *As palavras seladas (The sealed words)* (Galeria Diferença, 1985). In the last two years the artist who has served as his most constant reference is Giovanni Battista Piranesi.

We will take as an example three recent paintings, those of the largest dimensions so far produced by Calapez, which are based on three of Piranesi's works, and see how Calapez approached the basic images: these are, respectively, a view of an entrance to a tunnel (from *Descrizione e Disegno dell'Emissario del Lago Albano*), and two *Vedute di Roma* (*Tempio antico volgarmente detto della Salute* and *Veduta degli avanzi del Castro Pretorio nella Villa Adriana a Tivoli*).

In the first case we see the treatment of an inside space with the creation of a certain illusion of depth. Following from this, we are confronted with the representation of the outside of a building in ruins, where the walls are worked on in a way that negates the depth by creating an interplay of abstract lines. Finally, and in an exactly opposite way, we move on to a reinforcement of the illusion of depth through an enhancement of the value of the convergent lines that define the perspective.

We may consider that the fascination with the work of Piranesi is far from a coincidence and that, on the contrary, a brief reflection about the meanings of this connection will provide us with some useful clues for understanding Calapez's attitude and work .

The importance of this relationship has in fact already been pointed out by the French critic Jêrome Sans: "Si le dessin parcourt toute l'oeuvre de Calapez c'est certainement parce qu'il représente un moyen d'appréhender une forme par une ensemble de lignes et de contours, mais surtout car c'est une mise en place des principaux éléments d'un paysage ou d'une scène. Un croquis, une première étape. Mais recourir au Piranèse, c'est non seulement se référer à cette culture architecturale, à cette volonté, de comprendre l'espace ainsi qu'au désir de combattre contre le temps qui détruit tout et enfonce dans l'oubli des civilisations"[1].

2. One of the most obvious aspects of the Calapez-Piranesi connection relates to his drawing techniques, one of the widest, most constant and systematic areas of investigation and experimentation in Calapez's career.

Drawing lies at the very centre of his work process. First there is the act of sketching — the hand movement which gives an immediate, ineluctable physical expression to the most abstract intention or intuition. How to sketch? What to sketch on? The materials used for drawing and the materials for drawing on. The latter understructures have consisted of paper, wood (including the section of a tree-trunk), bronze, brick and more recently canvas. The ways of sketching vary according to the requirements of the materials on which the drawing is done: graphite, crayon, ink and also the incision movement made when the line results from a grooving of the crayon, ink or wood. The different combinations of these varying techniques make it possible to establish a basic material framework for analysing the successive phases of the artist's career.

In the works we are referring to here, we are confronted with the use of the incision technique on a background of still fresh oil paint.

The techniques used by Piranesi in his engravings and the corresponding results clearly provide

Calapez with a rich source for experimentation. The processes of construction, de-construction and re-construction of the forms through the proliferation of sets of lines, one of the main distinctive characteristics of Calapez's work, are also one of the reasons for the fascination that Piranesi's engravings continue to exert.

3. Another important aspect of the connection between Calapez and Piranesi is the question of architecture, which has a decisive and inherent importance in Piranesi's work, and is also fundamental for Calapez.

Architecture is one of the references and organising matrixes of his work; the architectonic elements are ever-present; the rigour of the construction and the propensity for the systematic are always in the background. This is a manifestation of a fondness for the geometrical which always ends, however, in not being taken to its final consequences — which might lead to a mechanisation of the drawing, and its reduction to computer-defined formal combinations. The geometry vanishes and gives way to the free mediation of the hand movement; the rêverie asserts itself and the drawing wanders, nurturing the tension between the systematic and the improvised.

The strictly speaking solely architectonic elements are always apparent, either in isolation, outside any explanatory landscape context, or in combination, according to a logic of drawing that has no precise relevance to the level of representation.

The processes of autonomisation, fragmentation and superimposition bring to us constructions floating in isolation on the surface of the understructure, paths, perspectives, façades, points of escape, which reciprocally contradict and negate themselves, ruling out any hypothesis of a stable, total or completed landscape.

They are pieces of architecture which neither make a city nor constitute a coherent, circumscribed, habitable place, a place that could be described as one of a conventional community. They are fragments, ruins, traces of longed for or lost places.

Being, on account of their decontextualisation, pieces of architecture without a city, they can be regarded as scenographies, especially since Calapez often structures the space as if it was a piece of scenery. The scenographic logic encompasses not only the architectonic fragments but also certain sets of objects which could be said to serve as props or objects of a scene.

Once again, however, this is a residual scenography, one that has been abandoned by the actors, narrative and drama that may at some time have inhabited it, remains of the constructions that in past times welcomed and accommodated the life of a now deserted stage.

The world drawn here could be said to be one without humanity, sustaining itself only through the authority of the movements of the draughtsman, but it nonetheless, and this is its specific effect, continues to make the memory and desire of a place vibrate. The place of primordial things is evoked as a place of resistance against the emptiness of the world.

4. Finally, and probably most importantly, it is possible to compare the historical periods in which the two artists were working, their position in relation to the past, and the result of this for an understanding of the respective situations of the art and artist, his historical attitude and role. Both periods are ones of transition between what is no longer and what has not yet happened, in which there is an obvious need to experience revisitation, re-vision and re-contemporisation of the pasts as a condition of again making the present thinkable and the future possible.

In his book *The mind and art of Giovanni Battista Piranesi*, John Wilton Ney emphasises how crucial it is, to understand Piranesi's work, to appreciate how he renewed the vision of antiquity and thus made a valuable contribution towards the complex and contradictory processes of change which characterise an era of transition such as the one he lived in. "The life and work of Piranesi are fundamentally bound up with the early and most important phase of this intellectual ferment which reflects the Enlightenment in its radical questioning of established concepts in all branches of knowledge. Like any period of transition, that of Neo-Classicism was shot through with conflicts and paradoxes as new modes of expression emerged from traditional patterns. In this disturbing process the activities and attitudes of Piranesi help us to understand the intricate character of Neo-Classicism as the preliminary phase of the Romantic movement. The central phenomenon behind Neo-Classicism, common to all its diverse aspects, was a profound change in attitude towards the nature and uses of the past"[2].

This situation is comparable with the so-called "post-modern condition". In our age, characterised by all kinds of "crises" and "ends" — of painting, art, aesthetics or history — and by a huge range of "post-" and "neo-" this and that, applied to all the available tendencies in the history of art and aesthetics, Calapez's work can be related to an underlying movement that attempts, through the construction of new points of view about the past, to overcome the unease of a present haunted by the ghost of the end of the future.

Pedro Calapez's painting offers us tangible but abstract spaces, witnesses of a lost reality, incomplete manuscripts of a memory, interminable maps, transfixing our eyes, and which we have not yet learned to decipher. In the words of Eduardo Prado Coelho, Calapez's work can be defined "according to a very specific temporality that implies not an incompleteness involving the waiting for a God to complete it, but a structurally uncompleted space that is concerned with the decisive question of a God who has definitively left"[3].

Translated by *David Alan Prescott*

Alexandre Melo

[1] Catalogue, *Chapelle de La Salpêtrière*, 1993.

[2] John Wilton Ney, *The mind and art of Giovanni Battista Piranesi*, London, Thames and Hudson, 1978.

[3] *Expresso*, 19/4/88.

Pedro Calapez, Untitled, 1994
Oil on canvas
300 x 330 cm
Photo: Laura Castro Caldas and Paulo Cintra

Pedro Calapez, Untitled, 1994
Oil on canvas
300 x 330 cm
Photo: Laura Castro Caldas and Paulo Cintra

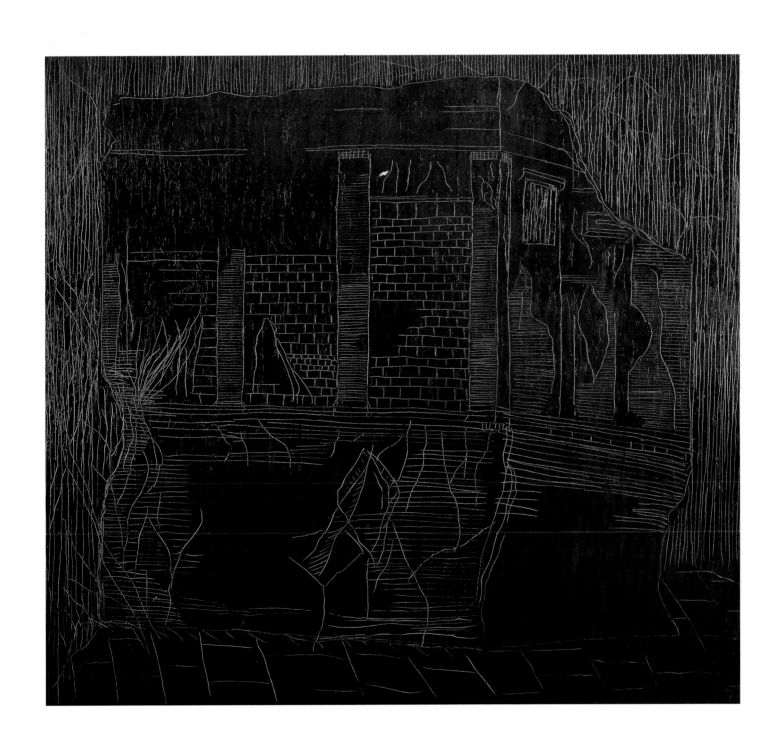

TARO CHIEZO

Born 1962, Tokyo
Lives and works in Tokyo and New York

DIARY FOR THE DAY AFTER TOMORROW

THE DAY BEFORE YESTERDAY — OCCIDENT

Modern man establishes himself as a fully developed subject through reflection and tries to extend this self into the future and the outside world. However, if this does not result in capitalistic accumulation or imperialistic warfare, it will probably lead to the utmost extreme of self-purification, the annihilation of the self, and the final artistic consummation that accompanies this: death.

YESTERDAY — AMERICA

Then "history"as the history of conflict (though it may not necessarily be so) will end, and mankind, released from the tension of history and dozing in material sufficiency, will no longer be a subject in the true meaning of the word and will degenerate into what Alexandre Kojevehas called the "American animal". Human beings will simply believe they are the subject while simulating the Hollywood models: macho men, feminine women, etc. At the same time, art will also die. But the logic of the division of labor which underpins industrial capitalism will be applied in the field of culture, and modernism as the purification of genre (even if it is not post-modern it is already post-historical) will be developed as an almost wholly automatised movement.

TODAY — JAPAN

However, after the end of "history", it will be difficult to sustain the myth of the subject, even if economic growth acts as a substitute for history for a while. In the consumer society based on post-industrial capitalism and eclectic post-modern culture, the absence of subject and loss of meaning will be clearly affirmed. People will become what Kojeve calls "Japanise snobs", constantly absorbed in a game of hollow symbols. Excessive sophistication and increasing childishness will advance apace and our TV screens will be filled with mutually indistinguishable beautiful young men and women singing and dancing perfectly like androids. Taro Chiezo's headless dolls are nothing other than an allegory suggesting where this process is leading.

TOMORROW

AFTER TOMORROW — ANYWHERE

But the endless round dance of those dolls, mechanical and yet somehow filled with animal vitality, is not merely a negative of the world of subject and meaning or an afterimage of the world of simulacra. It is also announces the arrival of something else — the acephalous machines evoke the aimless conflict of living and, within this, evolution through the survival of the fittest. In fact, even after the practice of a subject aiming at a future goal had been abandoned in other fields, the use of an optimal method to realize a given aim still remained the accepted formula in the field of technology. However, as the problems became more complex, the prior determination of the optimal method exceeded the limits of calculation and it became apparent that it was quicker simply to get started and proceed by trial and error. And even in computers it seems that the battle of the survival of the fittest is waged by competing algorithms. But then living things were not designed according to an aim in the first place; various genetic information must have been shuffled and selected in the process of evolution. The vectors of this evolution have by now penetrated the mechanosphere and unforeseen combinations of the mechanical (or "machinique", according to Gilles Deleuze and Félix Guattari) and the animal are continually being created, as the latest works of Taro Chiezo suggest in various forms. But what position will mankind occupy in this process? Will he become extinct or turn into a biomechanoid? We cannot even predict the outcome.

Taro Chiezo
Preparatory drawing for Calf-Engine 1, 1994
Sponsored by EC Japan Festival

Translated by *Richard Sams*

Akira Asada

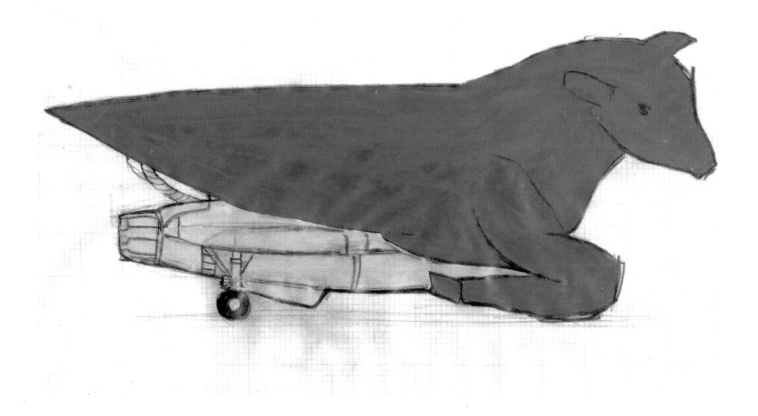

Taro Chiezo, Installation
Sandra Gering Gallery, New York, 1993
Courtesy Sandra Gering Gallery, New York

Taro Chiezo, Sink-Dolphin, 1993
Enamel paint on FRP,
resin, oil, paint, sink.
57 x 150 x 120 cm
Courtesy Cellar Gallery

JOSÉ PEDRO CROFT

Born 1957, Oporto
Lives and works in Lisbon

To appreciate José Pedro Croft's present work it is essential in my view to have an understanding of his previous works and follow the coherent pattern of his career.

In his early work he preferred to use stone, onto which, through mechanical processes and in the tradition of "modern" sculpture, he introduced animal figuration (embossed or silhouetted) in large, monumental structures (Galeria Diário de Notícias, Lisbon, 1983). The distinctive features of his work, the use of "architectonic" reference and the potential evocation of magical forces, were already discernible in 1984 in his installation at Cape Espichel, six columns composed of marble blocks demarcating a large circular space, judiciously positioned at the edge of a promontory. The motifs sculpted in the stone (relating to a pre- or proto-historically inspired iconography), the layout of the installation (a circle resonant of megalithic times) and the place chosen (one of the Portuguese maritime capes with abundant vestiges of a mythical history), in my opinion reveal his interest at that time in the restitution/recovery of the "aura" of the work of art and especially of sculpture.

The column shown at ARCO in Madrid (1986) abandoned the monolithic block that had characterised some of his previous works. Its structure was achieved by the piling up of irregular, fragmented marble blocks in a state of apparent precariousness and instability, in a deliberate interplay between equilibrium and disequilibrium; this came to constitute another characteristic of his work, which I call "deconstructed construction". The work presented at the Forum in Zurich (1987) emphasised, on the other hand, the architectonic reference: the placing of small marble slabs in layers one on top of each other gave rise to a sort of sarcophagus-house on an anthropomorphic level, and established another symbolic and monumental dimension (the tumulary) in a metaphorical work of mourning that sought to give poetical expression to the integration of the values of death and loss.

Soon afterwards, the use of bronze as the medium marks, I think, a significant change in Croft's work, which tended more and more towards objectuality. In the 1989 exhibitions (Galeria Diferença, Lisbon; Galeria Atlântica, Oporto), he displayed small sculptures like miniatures of architectonic features and explored various possibilities: the relationships between the outer and inner; the circulation of energy within an enclosed area (a ball at the centre of a rectangle), and the paradoxical, self-contained enclosed spaces (a walled circle in the middle of which he installed what seemed to be the roof of a small house). He was aiming at the restitution of the "aura", that was strongly released by this set of sculptures, in which Croft is searching for essential configurations in the formal construction, with chaos as the starting point (for example, a volute arising from a formless accumulation), or the *double aura of the vestige of the vestige* (José Gil). The white-painted bronze that appears in some of the works is another expressive vector systematically explored by the artist; the colour white is deliberately used to detract from the implicit monumentality of the bronze, to eliminate the solemnity of the art and at the same time confer on it that "primary intensity" that the objects possessed when they were still nothing more nor less than plaster casts.

This "primary intensity" I am referring to is even more clearly pursued in his works in 1990 (Galeria Alda Cortez, Lisbon) and 1991 (Galeria Atlântica, Oporto), where the form itself is above all the investigation of a principle, an "arche". Objects with such commonplace forms as chamber-pots, shelves, arches and chimneys are thus subjected to a deconstruction treatment, the aim of which is to achieve the primordial construction; the casting work is therefore inverted, and the final form is not the result of a cast, since the cast is what asserts itself as the paradigm of the final object. The sculpture is the shadow of the Platonic cave (Filomena Molder), the shadow of a world that is real but to which we do not have access; hence also, its immaculate whiteness simultaneously invites an approach, but can never be touched, as if it was the pure world of ideas that was being presented.

Sculptures such as these deal with the displacement of meaning; what you see at first (everyday objects) is not what is really there. In the 1993 exhibition (Galeria Valentim de Carvalho, Lisbon), the meaning of the work was maintained, but with a change and contrast of scale: a large white tank, which could not contain anything, because it had openings at the side; a small earthenware wall basin, completely empty, which no liquid could reach. If the non-functionality of certain works (for instance, a bottomless, unusable bronze basin) can underline this paradigm, the underlying principle in the artist's work is most clear in the double effect on the memory, which is enforced by the uneasy recognition of each object: the formal memory is misleading, because it makes one see what is not there, while what is there seems to come from a distant memory where the object was still the "idea" of the object.

In his recent works José Pedro Croft takes as his starting point pieces of domestic furniture — tables, chairs and stools — and adds plaster forms, thus radicalising his thought about the functionality/non-functionality of the objects and at the same time working in another way on the problem of deconstruction/constructed.

The relationship of the plaster with these objects is always based on the nature of the piece of furniture itself; it is not really an intervention on the pieces of furniture but a search for unknown meanings they may embody; tensions and displacements these functional forms conceal in their ordinary everyday use, thereby creating new angles of vision and new fields of light. In his suspension of these objects the sculptor places them in a kind of no-man's-land between their functionality and their elevation to works of art (the result of the plaster forms that emerge or flow out from under the coverings).

The whiteness of the plaster always appears as an effusion from the wood and finally gives form to the object. They are sculptures between worlds and between materials, deterritorialised from their functionality and reterritorialised by a new, almost pictorical dimension that these smooth white surfaces confer on them.

Translated by *James Ormiston*

Isabel Carlos

References: Isabel Carlos, "José Pedro Croft" (review), *Flash Art*; José Gil, "A aura do presente", Exhibition Catalogue, Galeria Atlântica / Galeria Diferença, Oporto, 1989; Filomena Molder, "Sobre as esculturas de José Pedro Croft", Exhibition Catalogue, Galeria Atlântica / Galeria Alda Cortez, Oporto / Lisbon, 1989.

José Pedro Croft, Untitled, 1994
Plaster and wood
36,5 x 50 x 39 cm
Photo: Laura Castro Caldas and Paulo Cintra

José Pedro Croft, Untitled, 1994
Plaster and wood
82 x 117 x 180 cm
Photo: Laura Castro Caldas and Paulo Cintra

José Pedro Croft, Untitled, 1994
Plaster and wood
73 x 160 x 160 cm
Photo: Laura Castro Caldas and Paulo Cintra

José Pedro Croft, Untitled, 1994
Plaster and wood
26 x 63 x 63 cm
Photo: Laura Castro Caldas and Paulo Cintra

WIM DELVOYE

Born 1965, Wervik (Belgium)
Lives and works in Gent (Belgium)

A HUNTER-COLLECTOR OF IMAGES

I never lose the urge to produce a strong image... A strong image is like a nail going right through your eye.

Wim Delvoye[1]

A nail going right through your eye — a strong image for speaking about other images. From this statement by the artist we may at once deduce one of the characteristics of his whole work: the play on visibility, the image as an absolute. The works by Delvoye are powerful visibility machines, infernal image machines.

Each work by the artist shoots into the viewer's gaze; it is impossible not to see it, impossible to remain indifferent, impossible not to notice it: sewage pipes held by large earthenware vases decorated with delicate floral motifs.

To start with, there is the choice of objects that provide an immediate degree of recognition for any human being — pipes, goalposts, ironing-boards, shovels: these are the support-objects of Delvoye's works. In other words, one's eye does not need to have been trained by galleries and museums in order to *See* these pieces. But nor are they ready-made, everyday objects raised to the dignity of work of art simply by being transposed to the museum, for they have undergone strong intervention, have been disguised, and, more than that, they are objects coupled in strange, not at all orthodox, marriages: the social origins are quite distinct, if not opposite, the materials are not the same and certainly do not belong to the same world.

At a second glance, and for the viewer with a trained eye, the reference may or may not be identified regarding the decorative motifs on the large supporting vases (somewhere between rococo and baroque and seventeenth-century Portuguese *azulejo* work — white, blue, yellow — as background), the decorative motifs painted on the gas bottles (*Delftse butaangasflessen*, 1986-90), the heraldic symbols painted on the shovels, or the ironing-boards (*Heraldische Strijkplanken*, 1988-90).

Delvoye thus tackles the two modes of vision and perception that we have in relation to what surrounds us, as defined by Erwin Panofsky in his *Studies in Iconology*. His pieces are both the vehicle for an elementary nature, easily understood, in which the shape of the object is automatically identified — that which Panofsky called the factual meaning — and are simultaneously, and immediately, images. Images here also in the sense of Panofsky's iconography, that is, everything we look at and identify as bearing a secondary meaning.

The reference to iconography is fundamental to an understanding of Delvoye's work, not only for the reasons we have seen but also, and above all, because of the relation that the artist has with images of the past and the way in which he works on them (his particular taste for the 17th and 18th centuries is admitted and well-known).

But nothing would be more mistaken than to think that Delvoye is a Neo-Baroque artist, because what he in fact does is to carry out an act of terrorism within styles and periods. He uses the same motifs, the same images, in order to produce a counter-power. We might almost say that his works are, in this sense, counter-works: "...my use of ornament as a crime. I have the modernist awareness of ornament as a crime, I am aware that somewhere it must be a crime but, nevertheless I commit the crime[2]. From the avantgardes the artist has taken the ironic and deconstructionist approach; but the void, and above all the hermeticism, that the modernist breach introduced into contemporary art and into the relationship between viewer and work of art, seems to annoy him deeply. Delvoye's works are, we might say, a struggle against this annoyance and this lack of communication in much of contemporary production: "Pre-Modernist works of art are serious attempts to communicate... Modernism seems to have left this concern — and a fairly modest attitude — behind ...Condemning the ornament has created a new kind of ornament, non-communicative, abstract"[3].

But, curiously, it is not because Delvoye always works in a figurative mode where the ornamental is dominant that his works, beyond being powerful machines of visuality, are also powerful discourse machines: they open several, successive lines of reading, they allow the most varied conjectures, can be read in the light of sociology, politics, architecture, philosophy. They are not unambiguous, they are plural and impure, contaminated by several registers.

Returning to the visual terrorism carried out by the artist, precisely in the use he makes of the decorative and ornamental, we may further note that it results from an obsessive attention to the fragment, the detail — visiting a museum with Delvoye is rather like visiting a museum with an iconologist: he stops, lingers over detail, reads the object. But whereas the iconologist goes straightaway to the library to research the source of that image or detail, the artist takes it away for his work. Not as an idea, starting-point or element, but in a completely totalitarian way: he amplifies, maximizes, monumentalizes, makes it his, mixes, displaces.

In Delvoye *To see* is the same as *To have*. I see it, it's mine. And what emerges from this first approach to the final work is clearly an ability to synthetize, to agglutinate, and a fine visual sense. He is a hunter-collector of images.

But it is not the image for the image's sake, hunting effects and adornments for the sake of hunting, which really drives this Work. We can easily find, in the disparity of objects created so far by the artist, a series of ideas-constants, things that want to communicate: the relationship between man and woman, between the male universe and the female universe (heraldic symbols-images from a world of men, of the assertion of an outside, political power, placed on ironing-boards, household and utilitarian objects from the world of women; brutality and delicacy-tenderness (the net about to receive the impact of the goal is a fine and delicate stained-glass window; the rough, dirty, pipes are held by fragile, pretty vases); the building, work and idleness (the cement-mixer, the shovel and now the sewage pipes); the destabilizing of top and bottom (the *azulejos* with a refined decorative pattern but where the matter which is the source of the pattern is human excrement; the bodies-telescopes that allow the sky, the heavens, the firmament to be seen but whose eyepiece is located in the ass; or in the Lisbon piece where the sewage pipes that were buried in the bowels of the city are placed in an exhibition and raised from the ground by pieces of high decorative value).

The question of what is decorative, as we have already seen, is one of the most interesting questions posed by Delvoye's work; but more than the problematic of ill-relations between modernity and decorativism, it is of interest to see how the artist works with the decorative arts: rehabilitating what has lost its aura seems to be the intention of the Belgian artist. Contrary to Benjamin, Delvoye shows that reproduction — just as Warhol showed — can add to the aura. But whereas Warhol restricted himself to the mass-produced objects of consumer society, Delvoye works within art's territory. Decorative arts are the poor relation in the history of institutionalized art. What the artist does is to restore their aura to them, or rather, makes them lose, as he himself says, their "negative aura" through reproduction in other supports and contexts.

Beyond the different support and context, the artist moulds the decorative arts with ambiguity and density by means of a double axiology: his works set up, on the one hand, a pleasant, peaceful component, but, on the other hand, possess a latent aggressiveness, one that has nothing psychological or mental, but which is always rooted in the body. If one of these pipes falls, it may injure, just as the bottle of gas may explode or poison, the big long shovel could bury a body, and in the *Library* piece (1990) (a kind of carefully worked and turned wooden screen, from which there hang saws bearing proverbs) the handsaws are completely within reach and may wound. The works of Delvoye are potentially like the image American films like to give of pretty women: irresistible but dangerous, they end up killing or destroying men's lives.

Its relation to the real is equally — I would dare to say — perverse. Perverse in the way he makes reality non-real; what is there is real, it exists, we identify it easily, but it has been transported to another reality that is completely non-real: the fine, elegant vases are not for holding filthy, ugly sewage pipes. What the artist has stated about his series of maps (*Utopias*, 1988-89) is significant of this approach: "...everyone who looks at the map of Italy makes an association with a boot. With me it is the opposite. When I look at a boot, I see Italy"[4].

An inside-out world, constantly searching for the other side of the mirror, for the parallel world that we tend to ignore. A world in drag, as in the street carnaval in Portugal where men dress up as women without shaving off their moustache.

And this world is not the world of dreams, of free association, oneiric and psycho-analytical — this is why I distance myself from readings of Delvoye's work which see it as a Belgian outcome of Magritte's inspiration; if we wish to give that Flemish reading, maybe it would be more useful to go back a little further in time, to Hieronymus Bosch and to the Middle Ages, to a world with other worlds inside, to the bowels of the earth from which strange figures emerge, to women coming out of oak-trees, to fish with wings, to animal tails that are pitchers flowing with water. To large delicate vases holding sewage pipes.

Translated by *Helen Domachowski* and *Francisco José Magalhães*

Isabel Carlos

[1] Wim Delvoye, in an interview with Jos Van Den Bergh, *Flash Art*, n. 149, November/December 1989, p. 129.

[2] Wim Delvoye, in an interview with Luc Deryke, *Balcon*, 1992, p. 206.

[3] *idem*, p. 210.

[4] Wim Delvoye, interview with Jos Van Den Bergh, *op. cit.*, p. 129.

Wim Delvoye
Rose des Vents, 1992
EV + A, Limerick (open-air exhibition)
Bronze
4 Vixen - Telescopes

JOÃO PAULO FELICIANO

Born 1963, Caldas da Rainha (Portugal)
Lives and works in Lisbon

ROCK ART

If there is a characteristic which particularly defines João Paulo Feliciano's artistic work, it is the way in which he understands the function of the support, always presented in a problematic manner. Thus the supports chosen are as varied as the ongoing opportunities or intentions, allowing him to cross over through the most disparate languages. He stands out in the Portuguese field of the Arts through the association of sculpture with luminotechics, of sound with objects and of the image with technological gadgets.

This was true with *Stored Tapes For Future Taste*, a work clearly inspired by Duchamp, consisting of *a series of six jam-jars containing* previously-recorded cassette tape. This deviation from finalities, a formal recontextualisation, the recovering of materials, is where Feliciano's creative activity takes place, in the search for formulations which are everything but obvious. In this immensely ironical *clin d'oeil*, the music is doubly a content; it is within a receptacle and recorded on the tape, but we cannot listen to it because its fruition is preserved for a hypothetical future consumption. In its relationship with the two concrete supports, the music is dealt with as a substance, something which is not seen (nor heard) but is there *potentially*.

When, in the performance/installation *Crash Music*, presented in Beja in 1991, João Paulo Feliciano did nothing more than throw vynil records against a wall, he was again posing the question of the support: as the record-object is the support for the music, which is registered in a different time to that of its real playing, he demonstrated the fallibility of the register as a memory, as a *documenting* of the act. To do this, it was enough to show the violent affirming of another act which was equally or more directed, as it was particularly *physical*.

The installation *Minding*, presented in the Convent of St Francis in Beja at the same time, combined visual and auditive elements; on the one hand the fluorescent images of four brains laid out over surfaces painted black and lit up with light of the same colour, seeming to be suspended in the air, and on the other the playing at full volume of a *grindcore* soundtrack, a selection of the most demolishing style of hard rock. As sight and hearing were taken to stages of perceptive excess and illusion, the invisibility of the supports was established as evident, as the receiver did not have the possibility to understand what was *holding up* the various elements and how the whole *functioned*. Hence the ambiguity of the title, used in the literal sense of to mind/to bother about, rather than in the sense of mind/brain or mentality perhaps.

In the collective *Imagens para os Anos 90* (*Images for the 90s*), Feliciano has participated with the most sober and bare of the sound installations: a plasticly unsuspect magnetic tape, a simple support, entitled *Talk Show*. It is the result of his recent stay at the Faculty of Electronic Art in the Troy Polytechnic Institute in the USA, where he carried out a questionnaire with students and teachers about the relationship of electronic art with rock 'n' roll, and this recording is a meticulous and concentrated work of editing and addition.

White Dust / Rusted Springs, presented in the Galeria Graça Fonseca in 1992, is another case of a transforming *manipulation* of the primary aims of the objects: an identification of rock with drugs, after the mythology of the so-called "rock culture", by means of laying guitar strings on lines of white talcum powder on the floor. Feliciano's attraction for the *metaphor* had its greatest expression to date on this occasion.

His contribution to the exhibition *Depois de Amanhã* (*The Day After Tomorrow*), with the title *The Big Red Puff Sound Site* follows the same line but this time with greater implications. A large red mattress over which hangs a false ceiling with blue neon lights, with several groups of headphones attached to it, is the visible side of the exhibit. The invisible one is the music, played by the rock band that Feliciano fronts, Tina and the Top Ten. The materials are intentionally light, but the music is heavy, with strong rhythmical beats and accentuated guitar distortion. We might judge that the artist is working here with nuances of *weight*, the weight of the supports, and the weight of what seems to be the *hard nucleus* of the piece, precisely the music. This is, however, the only element which has no visible or tactile materiality, or rather, it is completely weightless.

Well, if the conditions of any matter, as João Paulo Feliciano himself stresses, are "energy, conductibility and electricity", if matter is everything that has the vibration of its molecular particles as a property ("smaller bricks, only", he says), how does one consider sound and its organisation into music, especially when dealing with music as energetic and electric as rock? The doubt has a solution, considered under the viewpoint, as has happened in his earlier installations, of the greater or lesser substantiality of not only that which is material but also that which *cries out* its immateriality. Etymologically, a substance is "that which is underneath", that which is covered or wrapped up. Thus, the substance is inaccessible to the senses, only being obtained through an abstraction from sensitive things.

Equally interesting is the superimposing of the social experience over something which we would only naively accept as a self-explanatory aesthetic experience. If the headphones determine the egoism of listening to music, even symbolising modern man's individualism, the fact that so many sets of headphones are available to the visitor is a *trap*. The mattress is a support for the action, supposing that anyone who wants to listen to the music would lie on it, given that there is no other *use* for the work apart from that of the performance. There is a humorous aspect in the motivations one may guess at, with a reference to group sex, of course: each person will have to make decisions, either opting or not to place themselves among the other reclining bodies. The sustaining of the *accident* is proper to a support, and the game provided by *The Big Red Puff* provides us with some behavioural analysis.

It is worth stressing, also, the magical allusions of this sound installation, which refers us particularly to the Tibetan Buddhist conception of music. The mattress represents earth, and the false ceiling, emitting blue light, the sky, and just as the telescopic trumpets played by the monks of Tibet guarantee the harmony of the world, with their deep and low dronings, the guitar feedback produces the sound necessary to *complete* everything. In fact, it is João Paulo Feliciano's intention that the user of his piece should feel as if *floating*, in a state of consciousness which, without being contemplative, as it requires his active intervention, is conditioned on the sensory level by the surrounding setup and the position of the body. The magician is he who has the property to *change*.

Rock, by nature poor in aesthetical investment, is elevated in this installation, as in other creations by Feliciano, to an importance which cancels out the distinction between high and low cultures, between "art for art's sake" and popular art. It is curious to notice that the greater complexity of this *Sound Site*, one of the several that the guitarist and artist intends to set up, resides in the musical construction itself. The visual supports are simple and elementary; the music is that which is more elaborate. Besides, Tina and The Top Ten are known in the music field as a group which plays an elaborate and challenging type of rock, paying attention to experimentation. *Rock art?*

Translated by *David Alan Prescott*

Rui Eduardo Paes

João Paulo Feliciano
Installation project-drawing
The Big Red Puff Sound Site, 1994
With Tina and the Top Ten
(installation music writers)
Photo: Darin Pappas

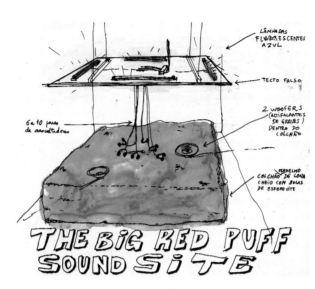

João Paulo Feliciano
Sweet Music, 1992
Installation
Mousonturm, Frankfurt
7 " Singles, candies

Born 1958, Maputo
Lives and works in Lisbon

Gare Marítima da Rocha do Conde
de Óbidos, departure lounge (Lisbon)

There are conditions when it is conceivable to be between places, or to be no place at all. Not displaced, even, but quite without place. In such a place, in the Departure Lounge, the traveller becomes complicit with the conditions of journeying. Place is suspended temporarily in order to reach out to another place.

Who knows where he or she — say in this instance she — is, or might be?

But in the Departure Lounge she knows and can see where she is. She looks out to sea. And yet, whilst looking, she is not upon the sea, or upon the river leading to the sea, but anticipates a journey.

Ângela Ferreira's work anticipates the journey in more ways that one, without enactment, without reaching a destination. For Ferreira creates intermediate objects, reference points with their points of reference, in turn. Sculptural relics cite the object(s) of sculpture, and are themselves sited in place and time. To *cite* and to *site* here become bound together as a dual action of presence and absence. There is no object without a presence and any history denotes an absence.

We are, again, in Departure Lounge; at the turning point of history. At the point of one history turning into another. We are in the Old World, looking with new eyes, somewhat uncomfortably, at the New.

These reconstituting (not reconstuted) objects cannot exist except by constant intervention and reappraisal. They all but revert to their point of reference (point of departure) and objective presence (point of arrival). The new version of the work allows for perspective on the history of the object and of the history of our relationship to it. In other words, I see the object in relation to where *I* and it *it* once were.

In Ângela Ferreira's work such a relation is the anxiety of Modernism. That particular history was a rhetoric of historical presence. It is here where contemporary rhetoric takes two steps ahead of itself to cite a position in the *always-near* future where the dust *will have* settled — what is called here *The Day After Tomorrow*.

Such citations for Ferreira are not subject to a direct anxiety of influence, from one object, or maker, to another. Rather, they are subject to the trajectory of time, when that original object of contemplation is so self-consciously wrought as to enter immediately into the history of Modernism, even before being visible as a physical entity. The object is so rhetorically historicised it is unseeable as anything other than an attribute of history.

The original object of contemplation, or source material, then, is not about its didactic subject (surface) matter: the murals of José Almada Negreiros fade into *example*, languish in a *pseudo--Modernism*. As monuments to an untenable ideology, these images offer no perspective to render themselves visible to their viewer they have ceased to function as images. No longer describing in the manner they once so resolutely sought to do, they are now only impressions or shadows of their former selves.

To manufacture objects after unseeable, politically unusable images is to acknowledge the inevitability of a Modernist trajectory, and to place oneself — however tentatively — at some apex along that line. But, again, influence is not at stake here. Ferreira's work is a reiteration of a site of stasis, operating in the field of flux which surrounds it, pointing to what it is not, to the centre it lacks.

The field of vision is subject to change and, indeed, to be perceived as such (to be *frameable*), must operate, as Joyce said, in an "ineluctable modality". What stays in its place — what remains consistent to its own mass — is what will eventually become invisible. There will be lacunae, or blind spots, in the field of vision. It may be argued that the blind spot occurs with the presentation of the object. That is, an (over-) assertion is made on its behalf. This disclosure compensates for that object's arbitrary position in the world. It has no place, and is, as yet, in no place. It is siteless.

The converse resolution to this impasse of vision may be seen in Ferreira's recent projects — *Sites and Services* and *Marquises*. Both of these bodies of work respond to types of sitelessness, without reproducing a sitelessness in themselves. The blind spot in question occurs in an arbitrary positioning which has *already taken place*.

Ferreira's repositioning, then, must be read as an ethical intervention. For both projects simulate a form of secondary *bricolage* as a means of formal composition. In *Sites and Services*, particularly, the process of assemblage is primary, to the extent that it occurs of necessity, but the foundation, or social order upon which their intervention or interruption takes place, is an external application. The provision of order problematises ontological solutions. It interrupts the flow, seeking a moral invisibility, but becoming only too visible. *Marquises*, on the other hand, exists as a supplement to primary provisions at a much later stage of development. Ferreira observes the consequences of familiar blindness. Fabrication, here, in more ways than one, is too close to home.

It may be inferred from these projects that externalised formalisations will always be subject to internal resistance. (In visual terms, here, internalisation is, ironically, what is visible on the surface of the work, and externalisation is the internal armature upon which it is supported).

But what is visible on the surface of the work? The irony of Ferreira's self-conscious equivocation in addressing the formal qualities of the object she construes is that it looks so remarkably like sculptural activity. However, the resistance to the formal emerges with the realisation that she is operating within a common or familiar language. Sculpture, then, is always a given. It is always already there, looking for a place. Indeed, its presence is too demanding, too central within the field of vision.

It is history as much ocular-centrism which burdens the inspection of the object. The object is an impression of something elsewhere. This is not to say that it is derivative or has no ontological presence or value of its own, but that the terms of reference, the points of departure, have always existed. They have simply been waiting to be defined.

In this way, we may understand a work such as Ferreira's *Carl Andre, Lever, 1966. Firebrick 400. Exhibited "Primary Structures", The Jewish Museum, New York, 1966.* The specificity of the reference provides a whole series of pre-determined elements. The siting of the work, and the citing of that siting, gives the new work a kind of freedom to exist autonomously in that very act of attribution. But Ferreira has not remade Andre's *Lever*, she has responded to documentation, rather than the thing itself, to create this impression of the thing. Although the Andre piece will always continue to exist, its form is mutable. Ferreira's impression contains the essence of its sitelessness. Her object of contemplation is not the object itself, but already the object at one remove. And even at that remove, the object is cited at a moment which has, by definition, come and gone.

Ferreira's solution to this double bind is to present something as if it were the work itself, something which masquerades as a new object of contemplation. Although it has been fabricated anew, the lesson of late Modernism might be that it is not new at all, but has been in hiding, biding its time, waiting for a place to be seen again, and understood as if for the first time.

Jerusalem, May 1994

Andrew Renton

Ângela Ferreira
Carl Andre, Lever, 1966 Fire Brick 400"
exhibited "Primary Structures", The Jewish
Museum, New York, 1966, *1994*
1000 x 30 x 45 cm
Photo: Laura Castro Caldas and Paulo Cintra

Ângela Ferreira, Untitled, 1994
Inox
100 x 250 x 100 cm
Photo: Laura Castro Caldas and Paulo Cintra

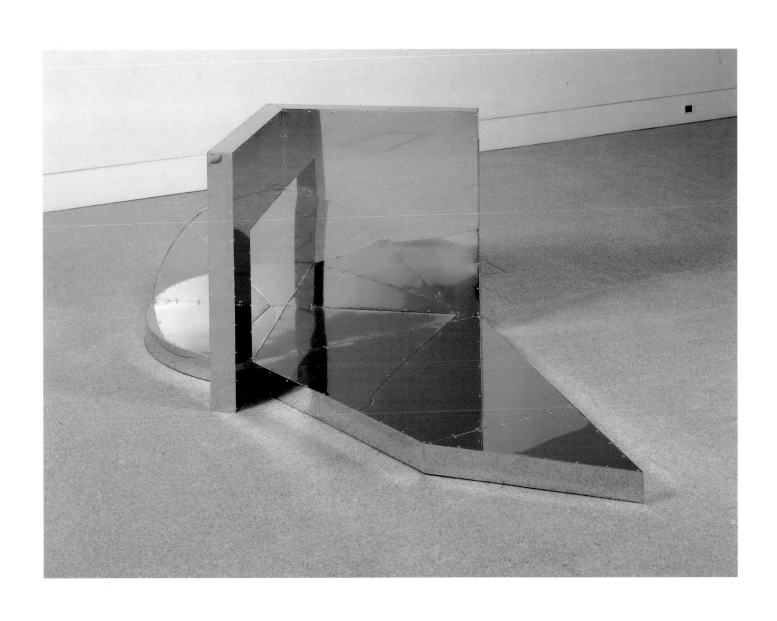

Ângela Ferreira, Untitled, 1994
Aluminium and canvas
300 x 100 x 250 cm
Photo: Laura Castro Caldas and Paulo Cintra

Ângela Ferreira, José de Almada Negreiros,
Emigração, 1946-49. Frescos.
Gare Marítima da Rocha do Conde de Óbidos,
Lisboa. *1994*
Cibachrome
130 x 170 cm

Ângela Ferreira, José de Almada Negreiros,
Emigração, 1946-49. Frescos.
Gare Marítima da Rocha do Conde de Óbidos,
Lisboa. 1994

NARELLE JUBELIN

Born 1960, Sydney
Lives and works in Sydney

"...FROM WHERE YOU STAND"

Convento de Nossa Senhora da Conceição, window,
Beja (Portugal)

Creating some sort of private space was an art, a privilege for some and a right for all. Topmen might do it in the shrouds, yarning there in elite championship. Or on the quiet stretches of the found, spaces to nap, to sew, to fish, to watch the sea. Privacy was not a matter of walls. It was a matter of behaviour, closing the windows of one's soul. Except for this, the essence of the sailor's existence was to be utterly without space he could call his own, to have all his possessions calculated narrowly, to be a totally public man to his peers and to be totally public to superiors who could muster him twice daily at his quarters[1].

More than anything else it is a case of mapping and naming. The European explorers of the New Worlds staked their claims with stones, boundaries and names. They were metonymic markers of a territory which had to be ever-extending if it was to appear to be place at all. Mapping equated to growth, to an elaboration on a theme. It could not chart the undiscovered, but became a metaphorical form of *recollection*. If there was any projection at all, it was to be in terms of where the explorer once was.

The map is the mark of the journey home.

Mapping is a fiction borne out of the necessity of confirming what was already in place, rather than the discovery of the new. Discovery is a trope for self-reflection, it is not usable *per se*, although it claims to bring objective presence or possession in its wake. It only sustains itself as an idea on the basis of its translation into contractual ownership. It is a kind of personal writing, and more specifically, a signature.

Retracing your steps, all before you is familiar and otherwise. As a matter of course.

The European explorers could not read the signs or indigenous maps as they found them. They could not read them because they literally could not see them. This betrays a blindness even to the possibility of narrative or dialogue within the sights and sounds they encountered. Such an inability to see the texture of what was before them is less to do with prejudice and projection (although much of both are quite evident in the histories), but it is more that this blindness occurs, initially, with an inability to see the discourse or trail they weave for *themselves*. They cannot read any kind of narrative into their labour of mapping.

You follow the track by the water, towards the bridge and its inventory of crossings. You count your steps as if homewards.

For explorers and cartographers, naming was a reflection of the self, a perpetuation of the pre-existent. There is a quest for renewal in the form of *remaning*, confirming the new by what was already grounded in history. What is transparent today is the kind of narrative that was unconsciously construed in the name of cartographic reliability and territorial legitimacy. This process of memorialising cannot acknowledge anything other than itself, but in the guise of gathering information, paradoxically excludes anything which does not fall within long-instituted categories. Some things, then, are literally invisible until an intermediary language is established between the explorer and what is explored.

You fall in with the sea, with your eyes fixed frontwards, and they seldom exceeding an angle of forty-five degrees from that front on each side of you as you walk.

The map will always reveal a narrative. It is not consulted for its precision, or at least, its objectivity. More than anything, it reveals where the map maker has positioned herself in relation to the rest of the world. From where she stands, the lie of the land will always be different. She will chart the contours accordingly. The shapes before her eyes will always have a look of her point of departure. Furthermore, that point of departure is not simply a place whence a first step abroad is taken, but it is also the seat of all the categories, classifications and assumptions which must be unlearned, before the traveller can really see.

The season has turned. The air cools these evenings, and the mist or haze of which you have heard hovers above and gently rolls off the water. Come day, the sun casts bright as ever, yet appears as if it were immeasurably further from you than it once was.

Even today, at the time of writing, the map is writeen in another language. Israel and the Palestine Liberation Organisation exchange documentation, but at a pivotal moment cannot be co-signatories to the same map. They do not see the same map. This is more than a dispute over territory. What seems to have occurred at the public signing and implementation of Palestinian authority is a lack of recognition of the map which was established only hours before. Yasser Arafat cannot see what is in front of him. He cannot read the lie of the land. It looks different in this light, in the light of day. Again, this is not mistranslation of terms, or of mistaken boundaries.

At the moment of mutual recognition, there is no recognition. After attendance and expectation, generation after generation, recognition is unrecognisable. Whatever territorial boundaries have been agreed and inscribed upon the map, the issue is at this moment textual. Upon whose map is this transformation inscribed?

The ground has shifted. In legal terms, there are no grounds. There is no way to map the surface of the argument, so two leaders hesitate in front of the maps which will contract them to each other. The maps look different — are different — in this light.

Yitzhak Rabin: "There is no peace without maps."

> *The shadows move around you their centre by perceptible degrees. You plot the course of the movements you will take when you can summon the courage to move on by means of stars, as a matter of course. You take account of the moon, for you understand its cycle to be a constant, where you are, where your absent companion might be.*

How to describe what one sees? The map, although a gathering or lexis of signs, appears to be held accountable to verifiable evidence in the form of visual proof. Mapping purports to be a witnessing. But the map is the accumulation of a journey, and to read the map with any degree of accuracy is to project one's own (intended, unfulfilled) journey onto the one that was once made on our behalf.

> *Fecing the bridge and the water, and then the sea, another ahead of you, who makes shade for you in the light.. One last welcome before you make your way. He still, even he, with open arms by way of blessing.*

At this moment we are not travellers, but live in the reported speech of those who are elsewhere — those who have been elsewhere and returned something of this journey to its point of departure. Even within the lived landscape we engage with the same kind of projection onto the map which we read when we are at rest, reading at a table, with one perspective beyond, from a single window.

> *In that fixity you fear misstating, misremenbering. You cling to some point or another in the night sky, for fear of losing your place.*

Looking out of the window, we read into the landscape. Or more likely, we project onto the horizon, the point of virtual infinity, the sign of an absolute elsewhere. We see absences, and perceive a lack of outward journeying and homeward returning. For the point of departure is always the point of return. But it is always to be an incomplete or dislocated return. If any form of return takes place it will involve a change and misrecognition.

> *In the end you will have come to retrace your steps, as ever, with eyes before you and eyes behind.*

So the mapping takes place in the mind. He for whom she has waited so long will not return in any recognisable form. At the moment of his leaving her, the terms and ground shift without possibility of return. He will not return as he was, even should he wish to do so. She, in turn, can only read him as he once was, as an image of himself, and piece together a map for herself of where he might be.

Andrew Renton

Jerusalem, May 1994

[1] Greg Denning, *Mr Bligh's Bad Language*, Cambridge University Press, 1992, p. 81.

MARIE JO LAFONTAINE

Born 1950, Antwerp
Lives and works in Brussels

Marie Jo Lafontaine
Video-installation model
«Il se peut que je puisse emporter
dans l'autre monde ce que j'ai rêvé.
Mais pourrai-je emporter dans l'autre monde
ce que j'ai oublié de rêver?»
(Álvaro de Campos), 1994
In collaboration with the Goethe-Institut Lissabon

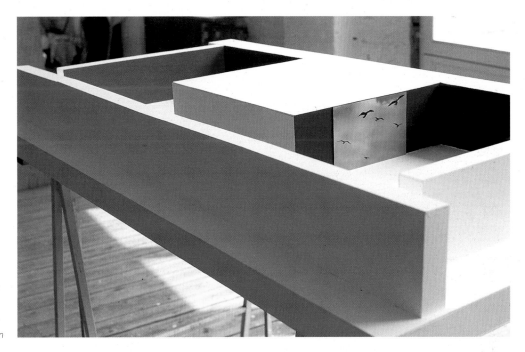

Marie Jo Lafontaine
Jeder Engel ist schrecklich, 1992
Video-installation
Nordijlandas Kunstmuseum Aalborg

Marie Jo Lafontaine
The Hip-hop dance of the waters and winds, *1994*
Sculpture on water
Wanas slot Malmö

Marie Jo Lafontaine, Wir haben die Kunst damit
wir and der Wahreit nicht zugrunde gehen, *1992*
Photography installation
Glyptothèque, Munich

CATHY DE MONCHAUX

Born 1960, London
Lives and works in London

ONCE UPON ...

Once upon a Duchamp, 1992, one of four works by Cathy de Monchaux selected for this exhibition, is amongst the very first she made involving paper. As such it plays a pivotal role. The other works here, *Safe II* and the two together entitled *Defying death I ran away to the fucking circus*, made in the previous year, otherwise have velvet, leather and/or brass in common with *Once upon a Duchamp*; *Safe II* features alabaster. The earlier works thus assert their tangibility and a material richness. The artist's use of paper instead pulls a visual punch — its whiteness tends to a confusion with the wall behind — and literally makes the work much more impressionable as it makes an impression.

Once upon a Duchamp suggests the medium of drawing — and as a "drawing" precisely is how the artist has referred to this work[1] — signifying inventiveness. Its title conflates a fairytale beginning and a name which personifies Dada. Paradoxically, a readymade introduction to one of the most detached fictional genres is in a short circuit with Duchamp and thereby de Monchaux challenges the ubiquitous tenet that, now beyond newness and originality, we are doomed to an endless cultural recycling. Instead, clearly, she believes that it is possible to get back to the drawing board, where invention is a priority.

De Monchaux has described her experiments, prior to *Once upon a Duchamp*, "drawing" with bodily traces on paper — lipstick prints, fingerprints and other smudges — and then foiling them with sculptural hardware. The infra-thin marks of such gestures thus would have been in stark contrast with supporting metallic structures were it not for the artist's conclusion that "drawing is something between the paper and the supporting structure, not *on* either of them. It's an expectation or [an imminent] closure of something ..."[2]. De Monchaux decided to make her drawing invisible, absolutely left to the imagination, to be unrolled perhaps or rolled up further into a scroll of paper. There is a restraint in this — not unlike biting one's lip in responce to overwhelming emotion — which actually is more engaging than cathartic expression. De Monchaux speaks of a potential energy, "something about to happen, or something that has happened ... something that has closed itself up completely, but [like a scar] it could still open up again "[3].

Once upon a Duchamp is notable for its obvious reference to earlier works by De Monchaux, such as *Grasp* (1988), *Track* (1988) and *Brace* (1989), which involve horizontal tubular format. These works are characterised also by a use of manufactured hardware, including clasps, clips and handles, not now a part of the artist's formal vocabulary. The readymade nature of such elements would tend to undermine her proposition concerning the need for artistic invention, ingeniously exemplified now by the use of paper.

Concomitant with this development in de Monchaux's practice is a more overt acknowledgement of sexual politics. The cheeky-sexy feeling of her earlier work has been superseded, to some extent, by observations on the societal dynamics that define contemporary male and female experience. She is particularly concerned with her predicament as a "late-twentieth century woman" — living in a world that doesn't seem to be getting any less violent, where AIDS has only just begun and honest liberalism is a rare thing. A number of works from 1990 seem to suggest a certain pessimism, with slabs of marble which are at once minimal and funerary, but rather than declaring a dead-end in fact they were leading to the artist's renegotiation of her visual language, to a point where she feels much more in control. Clearly de Monchaux believes that human (sexual) activity can be subject to the same creative process that must be brought to bear on a work of art. In a recent statement she starts from a description of her fears: " Fear of dark streets, fear of rapists, fear of psychopaths, fear of the male predator".

One is most conscious of what it means to be a woman when dealing with that fear. Women as a species [sic] are not prepared to protect themselves against the male predator — no teeth, no claws, no speed, no sting, no camouflage, no strength.

We have no animalistic sense to guard against danger, we only have our fearful imagination — always already making the worst things happen — the imagination keeps the danger potent and alive, the worst is always on the brink of happening, turning continually, every movie you ever saw, every victim you ever read about, every scenario you ever invent just for yourself.

So what is a powerful woman? In our culture it is still the sexual woman, the object of desire. Its strength is its very weakness, one finds oneself drawn to that frontal, pictorial apparition or aberration of reality, as seen in magazines or in movies. Alien to me and alien to women, it is other to both. There is no image for what I might really be, it is just as possible for me to invent it as anyone else. There is an optimism in that, a kind of power[4].

The four brass hands gripping the paper in *Once upon a Duchamp* have a *Terminator* gothic quality. Prosthetic perhaps, with claws and an apparent strength, they epitomise what it is the artist fears, and exacerbate feelings of vulnerability, while suggesting an effective retaliation. Such drama, embodied by the work, also exists in our confrontation with it. Visually seductive in the extreme — its materials combined carefully for aesthetic delectation — and hung at eye level, it invites closer inspection only to reveal its viciousness in greater detail.

Similarly with the work constituting *Defying death I ran away to the fucking circus* we are pulled and pushed around an idea of consummation, the possibilities of bliss and fulfilment alloyed with calamity. The larger piece, more than two metres high and just off the floor, resembles a cabinet with double doors. Luxuriously upholstered with padded red velvet, it proffers considerable tactile pleasure and yet the idea — forced on us by its scale and location — of being inside with the doors closed, or closing, makes it reminiscent of a coffin. It is a human equivalent of the Venus flytrap.

De Monchaux has made a container, a sort of a orgone box, where it seems one could be smothered by one's own sensuality. The title, again alluding to fairytales and fantasy, couples sex and escapism through the idea of running away to the *fucking* circus. But at the same time this work conjures up images of death-defying circus acts, particularly those in the mould of Houdini's — it is not only, and simply, a place to escape to, but also somewhere to escape from. Unfortunately, not everyone is an escapologist and for this reason, like *Once upon a Duchamp, Defying Death* tells a cautionary tale. According to de Monchaux, sex is loaded. It is a problem — now more than ever — but resorting exclusively to auto-eroticism cannot be the answer.

Formally more characteristic, the smaller piece of *Defying Death* is based on a template derived from the horizontal section of the interior space described above. Thus there are concentric brass shapes — halter-like — one closer to the wall and functioning like a frame, and two others tightly compressing a tube of leather in order to convey the possibility of some imminent extension. This piece has the formal intensity of a spring unsprung. Reference to sexual erection is as stopped as it is overt, and the artist's use of velvet suggests accommodation as well as penetration: we have a condom, on a whole human scale, which de Monchaux regards as being at once protective and suffocating.

The two pieces of *Defying Death* have a complementary relationship, and provide another sexual analogy — the component of one fitting inside the other — which is compounded by the unashamedly Freudian connotation of the doors. Being in the same exhibition, de Monchaux insists that the two pieces are not placed side by side, but rather located on different walls so that the viewer can have only a memory of one while looking at the other. The gap between them is animated by the idea of their connection. This is also crucial with respect to the configuration of *Safe II* — based on another work, *Safe I*, also made in 1991 — divided into thirds each with three virtually identical elements. Beyond coupling, the small constituent parts of this work embody the means and end of multiplication. The pairs of alabaster balls — contained, revealed and released (we imagine) — are foiled by a velvet setting which seems now particularly visceral. Vertically set, the balls are like eyes, like eggs, like testicles, like seeds, like peas in a pod.

This biomorphic quality is impressed on us also by the way de Monchaux fixes and locates her works. Their hanging systems are intrinsic, not accessories added later, and so it is as if they themselves are clinging to the wall behind. Like parasitic creatures they are implanted in the architectural structure that supports them. They are at a height for face-to-face encounters, and thereby imply a likeness to us. We scrutinise them as we might look at ourselves in a mirror. Furthermore, we stand to examine the work closely — as we must — with our backs to the rest of the room. This situation inspires vague feelings of our animal vulnerability which are amplified by the work. The title, *Safe*, only serves to remind us of the fact that we might not be.

That *Safe II* should be divided into parts, apart, and that these should consist of such contrasting and sumptuous materials, is not an unfamiliar strategy of de Monchaux's. The journey we make between each part marks the passage of time in a vital process — in this case, the different stages of an opening and/or closing — and the artist's use of brass, leather, alabaster and velvet reinforces its significance. Through this medium she makes it impossible for us not to identify with the process, although the snap-shut hinged metal structure (with nuts and bolts exposed) is resistant. The work suggests a presentation, but we are not simply being shown something.

As with *Once upon a Duchamp*, there isn't a nice neat story here, complete and self-contained, which de Monchaux has invented for us passively just to read. There *is* a story which she begins ("Once upon ...") but then quickly we recognize ourselves as protagonists in it, left to develop the narrative and to reach a conclusion. The optimism that de Monchaux has referred to clearly cannot be translated into "living happily ever after", but it does spring from a conviction that at least we can make a difference.

May 1994

Jonathan Watkins

[1] Unpublished conversation with the author, March 1994.

[2] *Ibidem.*

[3] *Ibidem.*

[4] "The Question of Gender in Art", *Tema Celeste* (Siracusa, Italy), Autumm 1992, n. 37-38, p. 73.

Cathy de Monchaux, Once upon a fuck,
Once upon a Duchamp, Once upon a lifetime, 1992
Brass, velvet, paper, bolts
49 x 78 x 14 cm
Janet de Botton Collection, London
Courtesy Galerie Jennifer Flay, Paris

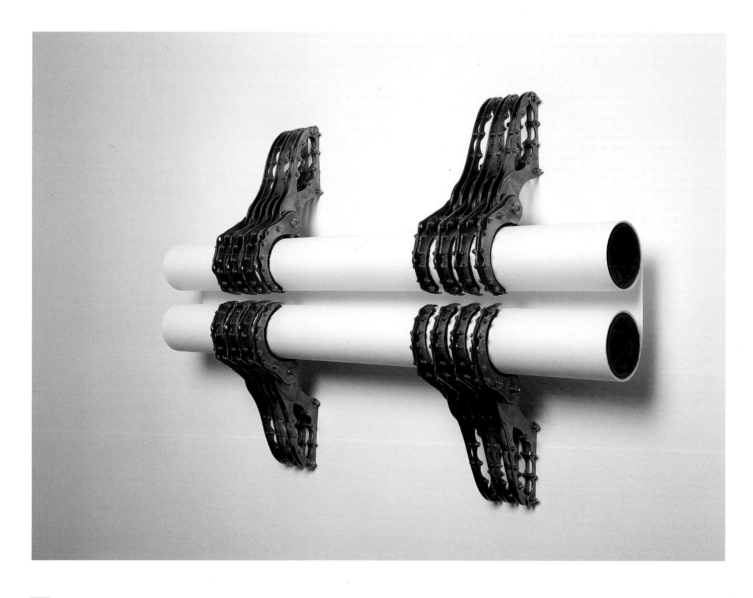

Cathy de Monchaux, Defying death I ran away
to the fucking circus, 1991
Brass, velvet, leather, screws, rivets, buckles
55 x 77 x 11 cm
Contemporary Art Society Collection, London
Courtesy Galerie Jennifer Flay, Paris

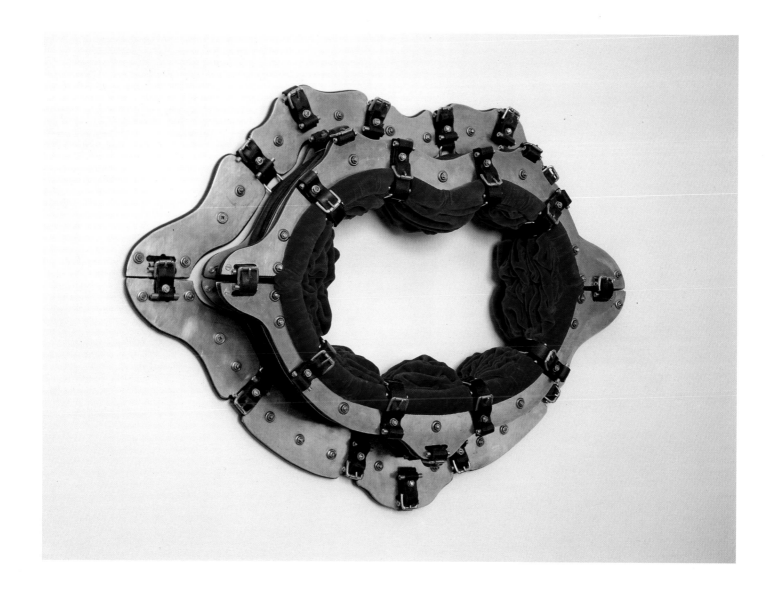

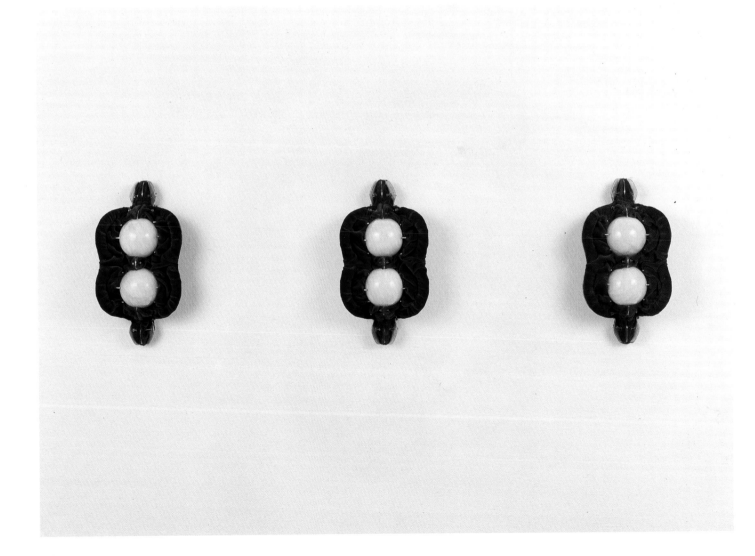

Cathy de Monchaux, Safe 2, 1991
Leather, velvet, brass, alabaster
Private collection, Bruges (Belgium)
Courtesy Galerie Marc Jancou, Zurich

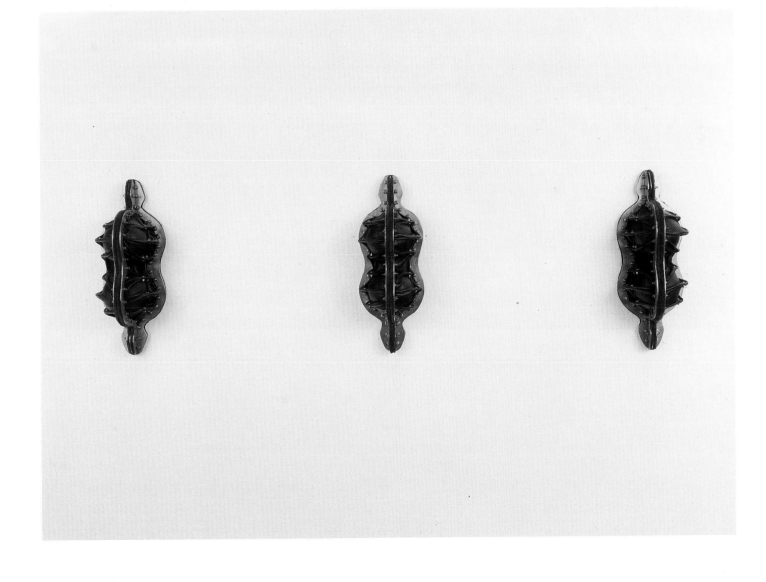

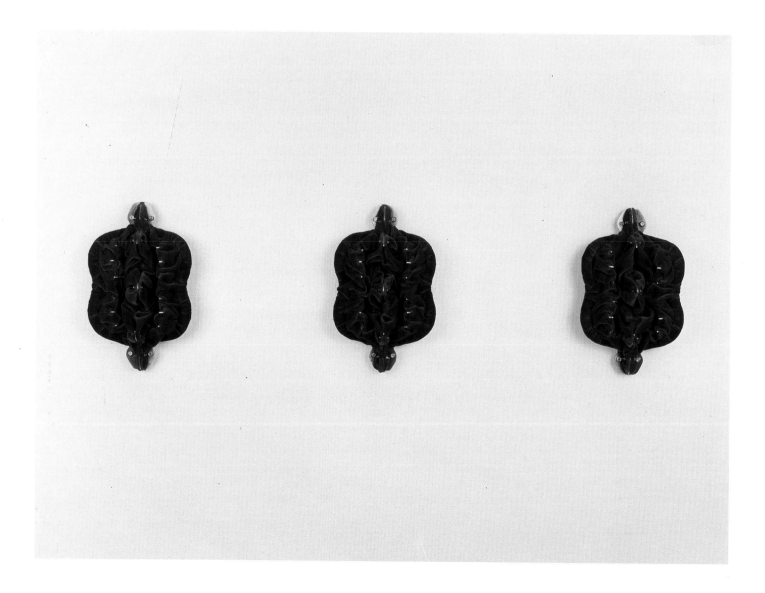

Cathy de Monchaux, Defying death I ran away
to the fucking circus, 1991
Brass, velvet, leather, screws, rivets, buckles
216 x 148 x 45 cm
Georges Guilbaud Collection
Courtesy Galerie Jennifer Flay, Paris

MIGUEL PALMA

Born 1964, Lisbon
Lives and works in Lisbon

A MILLION ESCUDOS INSIDE A SAFE

At one of the ends of an empty room, of about eighty square metres, there is an iron safe 1.55 m high and a 85 cm wide square section. Inside it a million escudos have been deposited. Just as in the piece entitled *Cemiterra-geraterra*, made by Miguel Palma in 1991 — a hermetically sealed steel box buried in the gardens of the Calouste Gulbenkian Foundation, inside which there is an iron globe of the earth — in *Mil contos dentro de um cofre* (*A million escudos inside a safe*) there is a content which is inaccessible to the viewer of the work.

The operation *Cemiterra-geraterra* was basically made up of a symbolic funeral. A 4 m deep ditch was opened up and a sculpture was placed inside it. According to the project, this should be dug up in the year 2000, that is, at the symbolic beginning of a new era. In its turn, according to the artist, this work proposes a sort of cultural interregnum marked out by a universe of critical references which simultaneously include that which we may call the "state of the world" and that which, within the same perspective, we would call the "state of art".

The modern world is not something we can be totally proud of. And art itself seems to be still penned in between a romantically-inspired demiurgical anthropo-centrism and the cheerful submission to the logic of the cultural industries. In short, putting the world and art in quarantine, suspending their actions, and above all breaking their ideological inertia may well be the critical translation of a project whose metaphors come from an essentially naive narrative source.

Seen from another perspective, burying a sculpture is to submit it to an eclipse, that is, to an interval of invisibility, during which the public presence of the work will remain purely conceptual, and after which the work will emerge as a somewhat archeological object, more or less corrupted by the multiple attacks of time. After returning from a strategic reclusion, *Cemiterra-geraterra* will then be a phenomenological presence: "My rust tells you that I was sheltered from human inclemency for nine years and that my return is in itself a charade. What happened during the time I was away? Was it worth coming back? Does the world still exist? What has become of art and my benefactors, the artists?"

Of course, if the globe of the earth in *Cemiterra-geraterra* stayed for all that time in the reserve area of the Calouste Gulbenkian Foundation, as happens with the majority of the works of art accumulated in the museums of this world (sometimes never coming to *public light*), we would never have the opportunity to see it again as what it really is and, in a certain way, will become again, that is, a living-dead! There is therefore a clear ironic dimension to the burying of a work of art. Just like *Cemiterra-geraterra*, a large part of contemporary art, in being expressly produced for museums, is destined for death and early funerals. The museum, which thus appears to us as the most seriously sought after tomb for current art, has finally become the place where the Hegelian sentence on the death of art seems ruthlessly to come true.

The work *Mil contos dentro de um cofre* produces, however, another type of *invisibility*. The safe in question is and must remain firmly closed. We know that a thousand notes of a thousand escudos are deposited in it, but we are not able to see them. In turn, this simple fact, given the objectified nature of money (which is in fact an abstraction of the value of things), creates a type of paradoxical reception of the information inherent to that inexplicable — and unproductive — enclosing.

If the safe were the property of a bank, the million escudos would earn interest as they were locked up as a bank deposit. In fact, such a deposit would always be a temporary enclosure, or, accepting that physically a bundle of 1000 notes of 1000 escudos could — following some statistical probability — remain for nine years inside a safe, such an imprisonment would still only be purely *apparent*, since although the notes would be physically still, they would *in fact* be inserted within a *virtual* process of economic and financial circulation.

Contrarily, locked up in a *work of art* entitled *Mil contos dentro de um cofre*, that money is condemned to permanent devaluation!

Of course, a future proprietor of the work could falsify the system, for example by putting a declaration in the safe, saying something like, *"This declaration certifies that inside this safe were placed, definitively, Esc. 1,000,000, financially guaranteed by a permanent and intransferrable bank deposit of the same value, in bank X, account number Y. The interest earned by this deposit should in turn be part and parcel of the work, although this wish has not been expressed by its author".*

On the other hand, accepting that the initial value of the work is at the least equal to the costs of production plus a million escudos, and that this value entered into the normal system of capitalist appreciation, one of two things would inevitably happen. In the case of the future owner of the piece not taking the million escudos out of the safe, there would purely and simply be a process of progressive depreciation of the capital represented by the thousand thousand escudo notes. But in the case of the capitalist essence of the bundle of notes being saved by the artifice described above, there would be a parallel process of appreciation, the implications of which would even be exemplary, in that it would allow one to appreciate over time how two processes of capitalist appreciation/depreciation which are typical of our era will evolve: investment in banks and investment in art. That is, *Mil contos dentro de um cofre* is, seen from a certain angle, an ironic model of analysis of the value of art in our civilized universe dominated, as we know, by the *homo oeconomicus*.

Unlike other artists (Bertrand Lavier, for example), Miguel Palma is not interested in semiotically dislocating the objects of his phenomenological permanence by placing them into some plastic surface which is essentially pictorial and formalist. His playful parody around reality leads him, on the contrary, to a confrontation with that which we may call *the heavy nature of things*.

There is a conceptual nucleus in things whose aesthetic representation naturally occurs through the weight, the scale of the materials, and the forms used in its configuration. And in order for this strategy to work completely, it becomes essential, on the other hand, to eliminate as far as possible the very rhetoric of art, for the most part inherited from romantic discourse on genius.

In the sculpture we are referring to there is an extraordinary tension between minimalist and conceptual aesthetics. Within a tradition going back to David Smith, Júlio Gonzalez and Giacometti, but also following the logic of architectonic space, we may understand *Mil contos dentro de um cofre* as a work formed by a safe and the open space around it. Between the two there is a variation of density which marks out, so to speak, the place and the time of the aesthetic reception. These in turn and in a certain sense take place on several time-planes; the time of their interrogative assimilation to the idea of sculpture; the time of the telescopic approximation of the gaze; the time of the imagination relative to the declared content of the safe; the time of the discovery of the space outside the work as an aesthetic space; and, finally, the aesthetic-conceptual synthesis of a territory finally captured as art. In one's memory there will remain, very probably, an unsolved enigma: what does value mean today when we talk of the value of a work of art?

On a plane which is diametrically opposed to the model of aesthetic reception described, proper to an élite, there are other possible and even probable models of reception. One of them, for example, organizes the process of aesthetic interaction on the basis of a singular phenomenon: the paradoxically unattainable proximity (except by breaking the safe open) of a million escudos. This is surely the spectacular dimension — in the sense that Débord refers to the society of the spectacle — in Miguel Palma's work. Through it, the author establishes a direct and immediate communication with that which we may call the *mediatic sensitivity*, that is, the aesthetic sensitivity which results from a long, intense and all-embracing process of formal and semiurgical optimization of the objects, discourses and values placed in circulation by the capitalist system of production, exploitation and consumption. The non-specialist public will thus tend to rapidly develop a scandalised, eager and finally frustrated curiosity towards that sudden inherent form of the strongest value of capitalist societies: the *value of money*. On the other hand, as the viewer finds out about the possibility of acquiring the work, if he has the wealth necessary to do so, the corresponding process of aesthetic reception will inevitably go through some moments of confusion and doubt, especially in relation to the notion of what a work of art really is. It is probable that irritation is what will remain at the end, but the accumulated aesthetic impacts will certainly last some time and, with luck, will stimulate in the viewer a *conceptual feeling*.

Besides, this spectacular dimension, which in turn accompanies the intrinsic and ironic functional uselessness of the objects constructed, has been a constant in Miguel Palma's creative itinerary. From his concrete watches to the race-car which travelled the 300 km between Lisbon and Oporto to be present in the exhibition *Imagens para os Anos 90* (*Images for the 90s*), there is a desire for mass communication in all of his works. As if, without the recovery of this old desideratum of art's, it would be somehow condemned only to profit from the many and varied vacuums of modern nostalgia.

Although it is strongly conceptual and politically demystifying, Miguel Palma's work presented in the CCB is not an ideologically closed construction. The core of the questions it raises runs transversely through the *place of art* and is perfectly integrated in the present dynamic debate on the contemporary condition of art in post-modern societies. That is why it is so stimulating, especially in a country where the most pseudo and pathetic demiurges continue to stand out as the aesthetics of power.

Translated by *David Alan Prescott*

António Cerveira Pinto

Miguel Palma, Cemiterra-geraterra, 1991
Fundação Calouste Gulbenkian, Lisbon

Miguel Palma, A Million Escudos Inside a Safe, 1994
Steel
155 x 81 x 58,5 cm
Photo: Laura Castro Caldas and Paulo Cintra

JOÃO PENALVA

Born 1949, Lisbon
Lives and works in London

Just before I begin writing about João Penalva he sends me a letter with a drawing signed 'Jean Buridan'. He does this all the time, making things up, pretending. Earlier in the year Penalva made *Would you*, a two-room installation in the studio offices of London art dealer Richard Salmon. The work was so full of incident and interlocking detail that to describe it with any degree of adequacy would require pages of text. To give you no more than a flavour of *Would you*'s overwhelming sensory impact I could point out one of the rooms was entirely lined with *pot pourri*. But anyway, that's not strictly relevant here. What matters, apropos this missive from Buridan, is that the installation included a letter from an interior designer recently engaged to redecorate Salmon's apartment, and three handwritten notes, one from an artist's assistant and two from his model. The assistant and model had worked for the studio's original occupant early in the century. All three documents could fool the unsuspecting viewer. Their language rings true, the handwriting is convincing and the paper looks authentic. But they are creations, gleefully worked up by Penalva as part of this larger, opulent ensemble. They are fake, but they work their seduction: the effect is real enough.

Two panels, one tall, about human height, the other of the same format but much smaller, have the title *Photograph and label*. From a distance the identification works. The large panel is a slightly blurred, practically monochromatic mottle. It must be a differentiated but coherent surface — water, perhaps, or the bark of a tree — abstracted by clever use of focal depth, exposure, enlargement and image cropping. Next to it a wooden frame contains a card which might explain. Close up, though, this analysis falls apart. The image really is abstract, being made up of ink blobs and watercolour splodges that have soaked into a sheet of paper. And the hardness, the smooth resistance of the photographic surface is suggested by the sheet of aluminium behind the paper, onto which it has been dry-mounted in order to get rid of the wrinkles. Likewise, the card in the frame turns out actually to be a photograph of water, the enigmatic shape to one side caused by Penalva's reflections as he bent over to take the shot.

Trio looks different. But then it is a function of Penalva's unapologetic capriciousness that all his work looks different. The word 'trio' denotes a set of three, but is made up of four letters. In the same way the work, comprising four parts, has three which seem to go together. These are canvasses onto which other strips of canvas have been glued so that their edges stand proud and cast shadows. All three are painted in the same way, their top half white and their bottom half red. The fourth part, which completes the work, remains visually apart. It is a letter R, deftly stencilled with sparing touches of tempera in such a way that it looks from a distance like a print. (Look! Penalva has even signed it 1/4). Placed second from left it echoes its position in the word, so maybe the collaged scraps on the other three paintings, in spite of their seeming arbitrary abstractness, also describe the letter forms T, I and O? They don't, and the more one wills them to the more mute they become, moving away from the idea that their internal composition can be 'read' at all. They demand to be appraised according to a visual rather than a literary mode, and yet even that is a precarious venture since their white upper halves threaten constantly to dissolve into the wall behind.

Of course, I think, Buridan's message has to be important. Penalva wants me to keep a fourteenth century French philosopher in mind while I'm thinking about this work. Or maybe it's not significant at all, maybe it's just another of his jokes. Buridan is most famous for his 'ass', a creature presented with two equidistant and identical piles of hay. The problem this putative animal faces is to decide which pile to go and eat since no reason to prefer either one exists. Penalva's art is like this. It could go either way, so more often than not it goes both ways at once. The right hand panel of *Doctor and Henry*, like the ink and watercolour image in *Photograph and label*, is enormously suggestive. Its dense, deep blue surface shades to streaks in some parts and in others is torn apart altogether to reveal a luminous white background. It is almost figurative, almost photographic, almost much else besides. *Doctor and Henry* has four parts. The largest frame contains a silhouette of a horse-drawn carriage. I have always thought of it as being a rear view, but it now occurs to me that we might just as likely be looking at it head-on. The far left frame has the carriage, without cabman or horse, seen upside down. These two are separated by a (genuine) example of the charts of progressively smaller letters used by opticians to check visual acuity. Beside the up / down, back / front rotations of the hansom, outlined but lacking any interior detail, and the chart (such things, too, are often printed in reverse, to be viewed in a mirror), the modulated monochrome might at least represent a yearning to see. Could it be a consciously-wrought depiction of the sublime impenetrability of the night's velvet darkness?

In fact, no. The thing is a canvas rectangle covered in indigo pigment which, when almost dry, had a hose turned on it. However the resultant 'painting' is understood, it has not been consciously wrought in the accepted sense at all. Penalva lists the materials used in his works in great detail. Not for him the catch-all 'mixed media'. Each substance used is separately acknowledged, and this is because they are all ingredients in a kind of cooking process. What he does is to deploy them, watch how they behave and then mix them up a bit. Describing this method of working, Penalva disarmingly tells me that he is powerless to do otherwise than agree to accept what appears from time to time. Naturally, there is much in his work that is actively conceived and deliberately executed, but the choice of whether to shape or to remain passive at any particular moment often seems to him quite as arbitrary as that facing Buridan's ass. (Incidentally, one of the things that interests Penalva about this formulation of the problems of making decisions and acting upon them is that the animal Buridan actually wrote about was not an ass at all, but a dog. Who decided to make that change and for what possible reason?) At its most extreme, Penalva's passivity has seemingly led him to relinquish control over the entire form of an exhibition. For a show in Oporto last year he displayed a variety of Rorschach-type ink blots produced by friends and colleagues. Interspersed amongst them were photographs of the 'Seven Paintings' of the show's title. If one desired to see the actual paintings, which were also derived from blots, they could be viewed on request in an entirely separate space.

The Rorschach blot seems not merely to be quite at home in Penalva's art, but to extend beyond that to provide a symbol of its playful perversity. An ink blot, somewhat like his work, is always unpredictable and cries out for analysis of its representational qualities in spite of its utterly arbitrary compositional nature. So apt is it, that *Crows feet*, a work that Penalva describes as a kind of self-portrait, includes a painted representation of a symmetrical, ink blot-like shape. It could be a commode, or a circular table, or some such item of furniture except that included in its outline are a number of (his?) facial profiles. Paired on one leg they set up the well-known optical illusion so that the understanding of which part of the image is foreground constantly flickers between the brown shape and the yellow surrounding area. This ambivalence also means that the yellow paint starts to look like a blot as well. In another place a profile combines with the cabriole leg below it to suggest a bull with head bowed. The whole thing, which stretches across six panels, is executed in a deliberate, flat style quite at variance with Penalva's usual subtlety of touch. Here again is a reversal, just as the legs (his legs? — the legs of a former dancer, light on his feet) seen in the panel above appear both right way up and upside down. Just as in the sign-painted poem that completes tha work we leap in a few short lines from child-like wonder to philosophical doubt to youthful questioning to crude bathos and tongue-in-cheek abjection.

These abrupt shifts are yet another aspect of Penalva's constant restlessness. The variety of form so evident in the works is bound up with his desire to test the boundaries of representational possibility. Similitude merely for the sake of repeating a successfully produced effect would, in this context, be superfluous and is indeed felt by Penalva to be a kind of failure. His light-heartedness, you see, is sincere and purposeful in its exploration of the somatic and emotional, as much as the intellectual parameters of visual sensation.

Michael Archer

João Penalva, Crow's Feet, 1994
Canvas, pine, newspapers, paper, encaustic wax,
graph paper, acrylic, ink, glass, oak and poplar frames
Eight parts: 75 x 105,5 x 4,5 cm; 80 x 79 x 5,8 cm
and six of 115 x 46 x 3 cm
Installation sizes: 232,5 x 473,5 x 5,8 cm
Photo: John Riddy

João Penalva, Photograph and label, 1993
Paper, photograph, poplar, aluminium, ink, watercolour,
glass and oak frame.
Two parts: 196,8 x 65,1 x 4 cm; 41,8 x 19 x 4 cm
Installation sizes: 196,8 x 112 x 4 cm
Photo: John Riddy

João Penalva, Trio, 1994
Canvas, acrylic, marble dust, tempera, graphite,
graph paper, glass and teak frame
Four parts: 182,5 x 140,5 x 9 cm; 95,5 x 71 x 4 cm;
130 x 97,5 x 7 cm; 214 x 122,5 x 8,5 cm
Installation size: 214 x 475,5 x 9 cm
Photo: John Riddy

MIGUEL ÂNGELO ROCHA

Born 1964, Lisbon
Lives and works in Lisbon

BODY LANDSCAPES

One of the artist's most disturbing works in this exhibition is the one entitled *Esquema para falar* (*Plan for Speech*), where a tense steel cable comes out of the ''throat'' of a moulded latex ''mask'' connected to a canvas box apparently coming from inside the wall. The title immediately points to one of the recurring themes in all Miguel Ângelo Rocha's work — the question of communicability.

Ever since his first solo exhibition in 1991, his subsequent works have constantly raised the problem of communicability rather than communication; they do not do this from the point of view of the mass media or collective communication, but (almost) always from that of communication between Beings — perhaps between only two Beings — united (or disunited) by affectivity. It is above all the judiciously chosen titles that give each work this dimension, and then the work, by its form, use of materials and special positioning in the space, begins to make sense, even if the way it is formulated plastically is somehow the result of to an absolutely original compromise between abstraction and reference to quotidian objects, between painting and sculpture.

Miguel Ângelo's Rocha's sculptures are narrative wrappings, conveyors of life experiences, as if the natural condition of the materials (in some cases) or their chromatic rawness preserved and retained the peaceful or violent energies of the memory, body and emotions. They create what I have previously called physical conceptualism, in the sense of the corporeal, material and sensorial.

In the 1991 exhibition (Galeria. Módulo, Lisbon) we saw canvas boxes subjected to various formal and material techniques using velvet and beeswax. The canvases were stretched out, billowing and rhythmical, as if liberating an energy rooted in the transferral of relationship problems (one of the works was entitled *Desta Vez Mato-te* (*This Time I'll Kill You*), the ultimate threat so often heard in situations of verbal violence).

''Le langage ne se contente pas d'aller d'un premier à un second, de quelqu'un qui a vu à quelqu'un qui n'a pas vu, mais va nécessairement d'un second à un troisième, ni l'un ni l'autre n'ayant vu. C'est ce sens que le langage est transmission du mot foncionnant comme mot d'ordre, et non communication d'un signe comme information''[1].

At the same time, though, Miguel Ângelo Rocha's works always convey a control of form which we could call perfect, or, if we prefer, they are rigorous and attractive sculptures. For the spectator they are traps, as they have a quality of seduction and involvement which at once, on a second view, is transformed into a seductiveness conveying aggressiveness. When I see these works I am always reminded of a phrase of François Mauriac's: ''Loving is the other face of hating''. The carefully produced canvas boxes, with their virginal whiteness, are subject to pressures, pulled and forced into shapes, liberating the latent energy contained within them. The titles serve as a discourse parallel to the work: ''Le langage semble toujours supposer le langage, si l'on peut pas fixer un point de départ non linguistique, c'est parce que le langage ne s'établit pas entre quelque chose de vu (ou de senti) et quelque chose de dit, mais va toujours d'un dire à un dire''[2].

Besides the titles, the contrasts between the materials-steel cables, stretchers, canvas, honey, glass, iron, latex mouldings — bear witness to this ever-present tension, the tension of someone who wants to speak or communicate but lacks the words or vocabulary to express feelings. ''Le langage n'est pas la vie; il donne des ordres à la vie; la vie ne parle pas, elle écoute et attend''[3]

These feelings are always physical and corporeal, relating to the skin, sense of touch and what is left by a gesture or expressed by a glance. *Que o nosso silêncio não seja mudo* (*May our silence not be quiet*) is the title of a work done in 1992, where the full and the empty were developed in formal terms, as a metaphor for the relationship between love and death, Eros and Thanatos. This universe now seems to impose itself even more explicitly and radically in *Maca* (*Stretcher*), where we guess at the body that had lain there and left its vestiges and strange shape; there is a tube or funnel to channel or evacuate something — liquid, solid, blood, secretions — through a slit that wounds the immaculate white shroud covering the stretcher-bed. In spite of all the digressions or imaginary adventures we may indulge in when we look at the work, everything continues nonetheless to be violently placatory, wrapped up in the untouchable whiteness.

These works are therefore body landscapes, a second skin, or faces recording journeys, sentiments and feelings, dialogues and silences.

"Cette machine est dite de visagéité parce qu'elle est production sociale de visage, parce qu'elle opère une visagéification de tout le corps, de ses entours et de ses objets, une paysagéification de tous les mondes et milieux. La déterritorialisation du corps implique une reterritorialisation sur le visage; le décodage du corps implique un surcodage par le visage; l'effrondement des coordonnées corporelles ou des milieux implique une constitution de paysage"[4].

Over and above all the interpretations these works may suggest, they are undoubtedly objects that create their own place in the world; this is why the way they occupy the space is so impressive, as if they were materialised drawings filling not a canvas but an entire room or the world itself, and establishing their own language and meaning. As such they are irreducible, being between the "seeing" and the "saying", or the "seeing" and the "writing".

Translated by *James Ormiston*

Isabel Carlos

[1] Gilles Deleuze, Félix Guattari, *Mille Plateaux*, Éditions de Minuit, Paris, 1980, p. 97.
[2] *Idem*, p. 97.
[3] *Idem*, p. 96.
[4] *Idem*, p. 222.

Miguel Ângelo Rocha, Plann for Speech, *1994*
Latex, steel cables, wood, enamel on canvas
15 x 60 x 96,5 cm
Photo: Laura Castro Caldas and Paulo Cintra

Miguel Ângelo Rocha, Untitled stretcher, 1994
Painted iron, wheels, enamel on canvas
117 x 200 x 73 cm
Photo: Laura Castro Caldas and Paulo Cintra

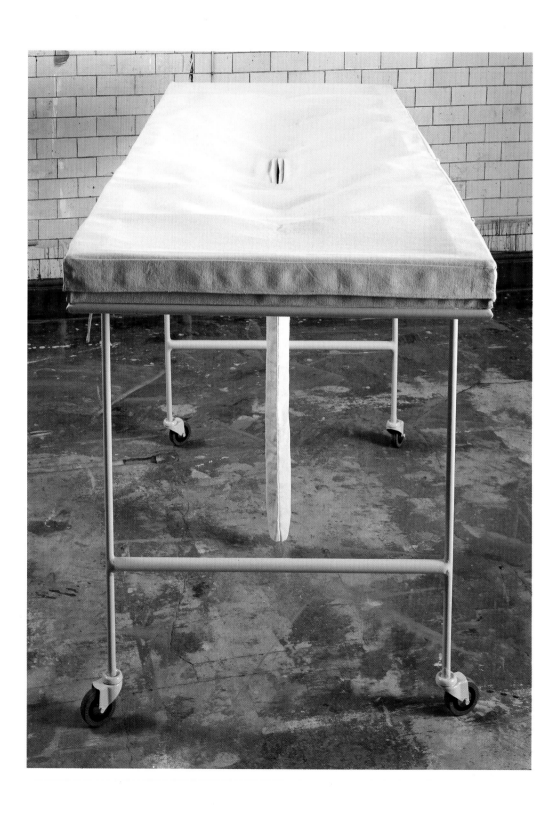

RUI SANCHES: A PROCESS OF CONSTRUCTION

1. Let us attempt to approach Rui Sanches' work through a very general text with a great and wide-reaching capacity. According to our thesis, the main theme of Sanches' work is the exercising of material processes of construction whose results show that the spaces, the bodies and the readings which they make of each other and the reading which each of us make of spaces and bodies, our own and others, are not a natural expression of being — of a stable and full entity — but are always the result of those same processed materials of construction. Processes like those which, forming Rui Sanches' work itself, are made intelligible to us in each one of his sculptures, and like those which he shows us in the works which, referring back to previously existing paintings or architectures, deconstruct them and expose them in their constituent structures, precisely to make the processes of construction perceptible, which, in their specific historical and formal circumstances, gave them legibility and meaning.

Contrary to what the dryness and the systematic nature of this formulation may suggest, we are not in the presence of a closed programme of structural description and conceptual analysis of the processes of construction of legibility, but, on the contrary, we are faced with an open and infinite game of permanent construction, deconstruction and reconstruction of the possibilities and liberties of reading. Any dislocating of the relationship between a body and a space allows a relaunching on new bases of the whole dynamics of reading; within a sense which has a parallel with the hypothesis of the infinity of the possibilities of interpretation in the field of literature and textual analysis. It would be a question of backing the infinity of the possibilities of reading of space by bodies.

2. The scale of the game is further reinforced, in accordance with the spirit of the contemporary post-modern condition, by the possibility, which Sanches exhaustively uses, of extending the confrontation to different historical periods and different formal codes of representation, with doubly stimulating effects in the reading both of history of art and its present situation. We believe that it is worthwhile analysing here the issue of the status of the references in Sanches' work, as the attitude implicit in his position in this respect clarifies even works which do not possess explicit referents.

"It is in the area of the classical (that I seek my references) but not a classical discourse. I'm not interested in working directly on Antiquity or even on the Renaissance, but on situations which are new. The renewed classicisms of Poussin, Zurbáran, Chardin or David. To work on paintings of the 17th to 19th centuries, now transformed by baroque impulsions or transversed by diverse mannerisms (...) which seek out earlier classical models, which appear as a display, as a spectacle, as something made to be seen, like machines for sight"[1].

Gary Dufour, in the catalogue for the exhibition *PastFutureTense* starts precisely from this observation to locate the range of Sanches' work: "The unique and specific historical sources for Rui Sanches' sculptures do not reflect an interest in or homage to the classicism of antiquity but to the new and renewed situations of many classicisms - those of Zurbáran, Poussin, Chardin and David. The sources indicate his desire to begin within a narrative tradition in which seeing and reading share a common ocular space. The sculptures begin a process of disarticulation optimistically propelling imagery, subject and materiality into the present. His conviction is that a language of correspondence will address the spectator as he explores the rhetorical aspects of display, spectacle, and the multiple genres of history painting"[2].

If we think that Sanches adopted this position right at the beginning of the eighties, we are led to discover a particular theoretical range in him. Post-modernism, or the post-modernist crisis, or post-modernism as crisis, have been lived out in fine arts particularly in two forms. The form of "liberation" through "neo-baroque" or "neo-expressionist" "revolt" against the dry strictness of minimalism and conceptualism. The form of "struggle" through the the neo-conceptual, simulationist or appropriational exhaustion of the theme of impossibility and the "end" (of art, of the artist, of modernism, of painting). The fact that Sanches takes works of art as a starting point for his work introduces within it a theoretical mediation and a conceptual distance. The confrontation with the historico-cultural period of the works which serve as his reference would also allow a reading in terms of a historical parabola and a commentary on current times. But Rui Sanches does not identify with the aspects of enclosure, tautology, struggle or renunciation which are attributable to the tendencies in question.

We would therefore say that Sanches has worked in the direction that we may perhaps designate, in a speculative simplification, as post-classical. In transferring the post-modern crisis to the historical and aesthetical field of the end or of the crisis of classicism, Sanches has made a detour which allows him to gain greater ground to experiment the modalities through which an order which no one believes to be absolute anymore may yet maintain the productivity of devices which allow him to open up to the impact which it would in theory exclude. Working "d'après David" and after Judd is then working within a post-classical exit from the post-modern crisis.

In the catalogue for the exhibition in the Galleria Stefania Miscetti (Rome, 1991), Bill Berkson writes: "Sanches uses history not as an orderly sequence of emblematic glyphs but as a reverberating field through which we thread our way to retrieve actuality pitched on the present fact of seeing face-to-face. Extending the ever-metaphoric leanings of Minimalism, he closes in on the heart of metaphor: situational precision opening upon indeterminate meanings, crystallizing our perceptions both ways". Giuseppe Canilla, in the magazine *Juilliet* (June, 1991), mentions the same point in relation to the same exhibition: "in the 'reconstruction', what matters is not so much the image which is the starting or finishing point, as the possibility of offering a point of view to the spectator".

Still in the catalogue for the exhibition *PastFutureTense*, Barry Ferguson states a generic position which may pertinently be applied to Sanches' work: "There is also a rational approach here which avoids the chaotic, schizoid characteristics usually associated with the post-modern and which tends to devalue it as a model for art or understanding. Instead of indiscriminate plundering or scavenging of culture to reflect only its apocalyptic fragmentation, an audience encounters, in the objects of this exhibition, a more cautious, restrained art which juxtaposes discourses in order to open space and time for considering the (past and future) uses and powers of the modes on display".

3. Having now situated the set of works done by Rui Sanches for this exhibition, we may now locate them in the most analytical, geometrical and architectural area of his work, maintaining, for example, a relationship of proximity with works like those produced for the Chapelle de La Salpêtrière in Paris (1993). The French critic Jerôme Sans wrote of these in the catalogue: "Construire, tel semble être la détermination de cet artiste qui à l'image d'un enfant, dépose des éléments et organise des circulations, des ensembles, afin d'appréhender l'espace. Habiter l'espace. Dans cette opposition entre espace comme vide immense et espace que l'on bâti. Rui Sanches bous entraîne dans sa lecture. A l'image d'un paysage, chacune de ses oeuvres sont des ensembles d'une plus grande composition que l'on peut extraire. Exposant à chaque regard de nouvelles configurations. De nouveaux points de vue".

In the case of the exhibition in Paris there was an explicit reference to architecture and to the previously existing aesthetics of the site. In the present case the relationships with the questions of space, architecture and the organization of the space is a more generic issue, although it still authorizes concrete articulations which are legible through the choices for the setting up of the works.

It is worthwhile stressing that the predominance of a methodical and systematical attitude in certain of Sanches' works does not preclude the demonstration of a correlative playful sense of experimentation, which is shown both in the process of making as well as in the type of functioning of the objects constructed.

The process of making has a primeval value in the attitude of Sanches' work. Making is a work of construction subject to the uncertainties of a manual adventure and to the risks of a precarious geometry. A balance between craftwork and geometry. If there is joy in Sanches' process of working it is because he joins the exercise of reflection-transcription to that of the physical experience of construction. Throughout the whole range of sensations and feelings which one may detect, for example, in the work of children who play at building or of carpenters who are Edenic in individual "unalienated" production. The sensuality of the confrontation with the materials. The experimenting of the substitutibility of the elements. The expectation of the risk of instability.

Sensuality is neither quite the delicateness of stroking wood, nor the "lyricism" of polishing surfaces. Roughness, unfinishedness ness, the trace of the operations of construction, even when they produce a side-effect of elegance, bear witness to the subordination of the work on the surface, the rejection of a decorative use of the rhetoric of the materials. The sensuality is the working freedom of the physical relationship with things and with making.

There is no exact previous rule which might dictate the form and the dimension of the objects. It is necessary to try. To construct one at a time. To see if it works. To rebuild. To change the strategy of assembly. To go back. To recover that which had been abandoned and abandon the starting point. The child who puts cubes on top of each other lives out the pleasure of the growing tower and the expectation of its imminent collapse. But if the horizon of construction is widened to take in a series of combinational possibilities, the suspense, without ever being withdrawn, may be infinitely delayed, multiplied within a series of possible, alternative, perhaps compatible constructions, perhaps not. It is not a question of spontaneity nor arbitrariness, but of a discretionary power which is close to a benevolent omnipotence. An attitude which allows the understanding of the choice of certain materials — wood, already prepared for industrial use, with a greater flexibility — the way of working them — piling them up and craft-like "carpentry".

Contrary to that which is suggested by the richness of his sculptural and combinational game, Rui Sanches' sculpture is not, deep down, either an internal game of shapes, nor a game between different forms of representation. Rui Sanches' sculpture, passing through the internal game and the game between forms of representation, is above all the establishing in space of an object which plays with the spectator.

An object which is achieved in the way that it redesigns the space in which it is situated, and in redesigning, as to itself, the perception of the space and the movement of the spectator. Sculpture, more than attracting upon itself the gaze and the dislocations of the spectator, redistributes them in many directions, throughout the surrounding space and in accordance with it. The body of the observer is sent back to the experience of his own way of being in space.

[1] Rui Sanches, exhibition catalogue, Galeria Atlântica, Oporto.

[2] The exhibition *PastFutureTense* curated by Gary Dufour and Bruce Ferguson, took place in Canada (Winnipeg Art Gallery and Vancouver Art Gallery) in 1990 and included works by Vikky Alexander, Kari Caven, Ronald Jones, Rui Sanches, Erwin Wurm, Klaus vom Bruch, David Diao, Jac Leimer and Barbara Todd.

Translated by *David Alan Prescott*

Alexandre Melo

Rui Sanches, Untitled, 1994
Plywood and glass
Photo: José Pessoa

Rui Sanches, Untitled, 1994
Plywood and glass
Photo: José Pessoa

JULIÃO SARMENTO

Born 1948, Lisbon
Lives and works in Sintra (Portugal)

Julião Sarmento, Laura and Alice (9), 1994
Mixed media on canvas
205 x 209 cm
Courtesy Galerie Bernd Klüser, Munich
Photo: Mario Gastinger

Julião Sarmento, Valenciana (2), 1994
Mixed media on canvas
190 x 220 cm
Courtesy Sean Kelly, New York
Photo: Francisco Alcantara

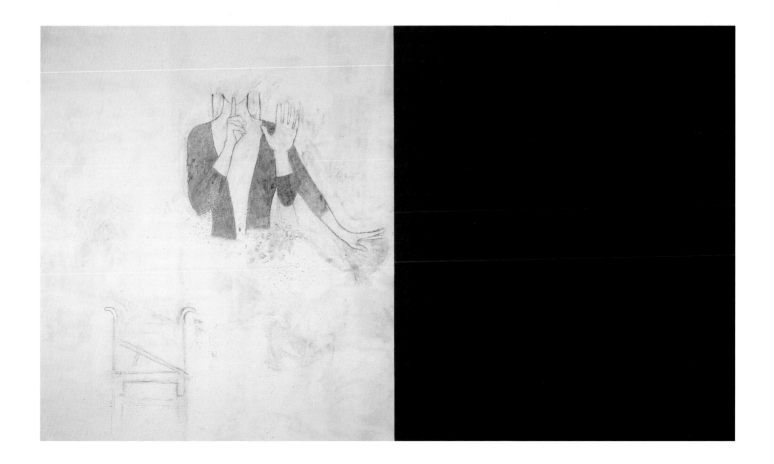

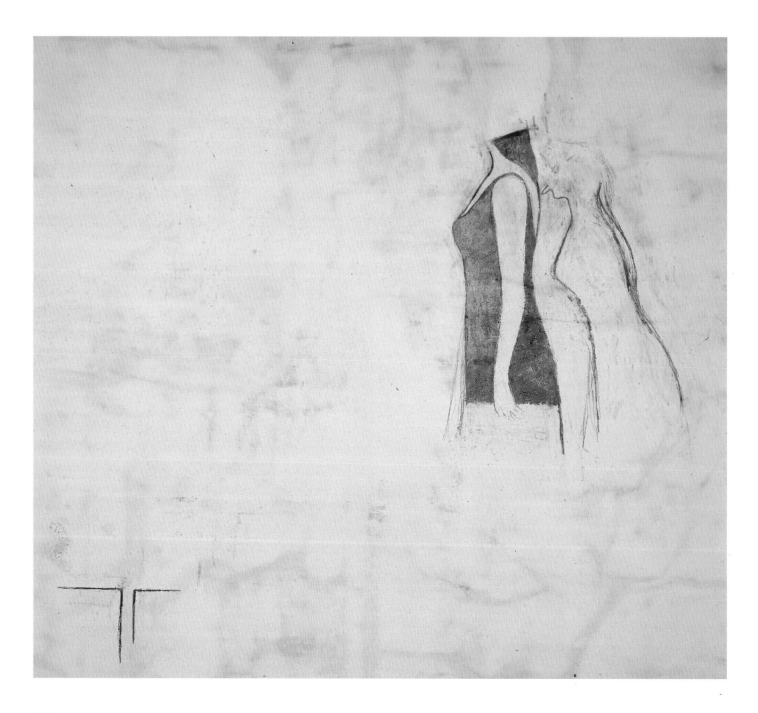

FRANK THIEL

Born 1966, Kleinmachnow (Germany)
Lives and works in Berlin

WITHIN THE PRISON NET

This text should ideally have been written by Michel Foucault, if he were alive. It would be Frank Thiel's wish. More than that it should come from an art critic or a photography critic — if this distinction makes any sense! — the artist would like the text accompanying his work in the catalogue to be written by someone who has either reflected on the question of prison and mechanisms of coercion in social terms or by someone who has lived through the experience of being in prison. Several possibilities were tried and tested: that of a man who was in prison for ten years for a crime he did not commit — the viewpoint of someone who is innocent, so someone unjustly tried by a system that is legal and judicial; that of a serial killer who had murdered several women — the viewpoint of someone found guilty and quite justly imprisoned; and the possibility of confronting these two statements. However, none of them could be carried out.

So back to the ideal: Michel Foucault. And faced with the physical impossibility of the French author writing, we tried another way of conceiving this text, by fusing two references: I would write, Thiel would send me an English edition — given that we had an issue of the catalogue in that language — of Foucault's *Surveiller et Punir* in which the artist would underline the passages he found most interesting and appropriate. Which at once implies a double approach: on the one hand, what Thiel chose derives from his experience; on the other hand, the artist, in selecting, takes into account his series of photographs of prisons in Germany and the words are also chosen so as to be functional and to operate towards a reading of his work in the exhibition.

This text is thus the result of that process. It is not a text written by four hands but with two heads, two ways of thinking and seeing these photographs: that of the author and that of the curator-critic with the present-absent figure of Foucault.

Thus, I would like to begin by looking at these photographs and writing about them purely and simply — if this distancing approach is still possible after a process such as that mentioned — from a standpoint of mere viewer-critic, but constantly working in conjunction with the quotations chosen by Frank Thiel.

The first thing that called my attention as soon as I saw them and chose them for the exhibition was the fact that the photographer, faced with an object and topic such as prisons in Germany, recorded only the gates and watch-towers of various prison establishments. That is, never the inside: the cells, corridors, courtyards, canteens the imprisoned women. I think the reasons for such an approach can be found in different causes. In order to identify them, the choice of texts made by Thiel can be revealing: right from the start, as cause, that this kind of approach to jail is the usual one in photographic reporting, through which one tries to make visible what is hidden, in which the aim is to inform and show. That Thiel should opt for an opposite approach — and from here I am moving towards a first conclusion about this work of his — lies in the fact of the photographer wagering clearly on a sort of *lost objectivity*, similar to that we find in the photographs belonging to the emergence of this language — that is, things are what they are, there is no theatrical staging, no angles that are formally very worked or fancy colour and photomontage. The recording is direct and frontal, the gates and watch-towers are photographed head-on, starkly.

Nevertheless, this objectivity has no purpose of informing the viewer about the prison world. It is rather, and apparently solely, the need to record. That is, what seems to interest Thiel is the prison as an architecture of enclosure, an architectonic device created by society in order to keep under restraint women who have committed crimes: "Through imprisonment, one has security for someone, one does not punish him" (p. 118).

Afterwards, we easily understand, especially in front of the series of towers, that the photographer opted for the prison establishments, closest to the architecture of today, "new castles of the new civil order" (p. 116). Nor is there, consequently, any archaeological or historical concern in this work. They are images which, on the contrary, show us how these structures have evolved, and where we can easily guess at the complex technological circuits behind those windows: film cameras, all sorts of detectors, electronic eyes that keep watch. The universe of the look-out post with the guard there inside, the human surveillance, is here something secondary on these towers; they are machines — and no longer men — that keep watch on the men who are behind those gates.

But it must be mentioned that in historical terms, and especially in Portugal, many prisons grew out of old convents (the case of the Mónicas Jail) or hospitals, and one cannot avoid reflecting on the similarity between convents and prisons, microcosms in which the subjects are cut off from the outside world and where life is made up of: "Exercises, not signs: time-tables, compulsory movements, regular activities, solitary meditation, work in common, silence, application, respect, good habits" (p. 128). Nor did the architectonic link between jail, hospital, convent, go unnoticed by Foucault, who writes about this kind of contamination between architectonic structures created for human groupings: "Is it surprising that prisons resemble factories, schools, barracks, hospitals, which all resemble prisons?" (p. 228).

Nor is the option for the installation of the photographs in the space without significance for the understanding of Thiel's purpose in showing this work: firstly, the tightly-closed gates, in a game that might lead the viewer to believe that, next, he will have the opportunity of seeing the inside, what is behind those gates; in other words, an effect of verisimilitude is called up. Right away, however, all this is contradicted by the presence of the towers, which, because of their characteristics, function as eyes-watchers that eye-watch the viewer, which peer at us, calling upon something threatening to our privacy as viewers of art. Another possible installation — but excessively literal and theatrical — would be in a circle, reinforcing even more the pan-optical gaze which they set up. What, then, seems to interest Thiel in a problematic such as that of prisons, is the immediate oppressive feeling which emanates from them. That is, the way they immediately function as devices of power and penalization: "How could prison not be the penalty par excellence in a society in which liberty is a good that belongs to all in the same way and to which each individual is attached, as Dupont put it, by a 'universal and constant' feeling? Its loss has therefore the same value for all: unlike the fine, it is an 'egalitarian' punishment. The prison is the clearest, simplest, most equitable of penalties" (p. 232).

In effect, the mere existence and presence of these buildings in the social structure *signifies* — it is not necessary to show the prisoners who live there. They could even be newly-built still-empty prisons, nothing would be altered. These photographs can thus also be the gaze of any one of us when we pass by a jail. They are the outside record of what any citizen can see and they simultaneously evoke something natural: "The prison is 'natural', just as the use of time to measure exchanges is 'natural' in our society... How could the prison not be immediately accepted when, by locking up, restraining and rendering docile, it merely reproduces, with a little more emphasis, all the mechanisms that are to be found in the social body? The prison is like a rather disciplined barracks, a strict school, a dark workshop, but not qualitatively different" (p. 233)

These photographs therefore wish to show or state nothing whatsoever in sociological and political terms (although this was the original starting point to these works), but only to confront the viewer with that naturalness, with the simple presence and existence of these buildings, of these architectures of enclosure: "...the meticulously sealed wall, uncrossable in either direction... will become... the monotonous figure, at once material and symbolic, of the power to punish" (p. 116). In its turn, it is not the architecture in itself which interests the photographer; what seems to drive him is, I repeat, the prison as a power device, as an object for "watching and punishing", its immediate effect of subjugation, and the effect of correction and protection. For those who are not there, for us, "free beings", prison protects us from the "others".

Just as a man wearing a uniform (and I recall another series of photographs by Thiel: *army guard regiment: "Friedrich Engels"*) looking at prison provokes an immediate effect of power. These photographs treat jails as symbols of power and repression, as badges or name-tags that are sewn, embedded into the social and urban fabric. And showing off a symbol is always more powerful and vigorous than showing what is behind it; leaving it to the viewer's imagination to guess what is happening behind those gates and towers carries much more impact than any photograph of a cell. That is what voyeurist television does every day and we know how that leads to total indifference and a deproblematizing. Power knows it, and is more and more ready to open prisons to the press and the mass media: "Our society is one not of spectacle, but of surveillance; under the surface of images, one invests bodies in depth; behind the great abstraction of exchange, there continues the meticulous, concrete training of useful forces; the circuits of communication are the supports of an accumulation and a centralization of knowledge; the play of signs defines the anchorages of power" (p. 217).

It is not life in prison that Thiel is interested in problematizing; it is rather, on the one hand, the ontology of being imprisoned: "body as security" (p. 118), and, on the other hand, how it is manifested in architecture, that is, how it acts upon we who are outside. It's no judgement about prisons, it's a reflection about law, justice, guilt, isolation; it is a photographic intensification.

Let the final words be those of Michel Foucault: "The prison form antedates its systematic use in the penal system. It had already been constituted outside the legal apparatus when, throughout the social body, procedures were being elaborated for distributing individuals, fixing them in space, classifying them, extracting from them the maximum in time and forces, training their bodies, coding their continuous behaviour, maintaining them in perfect visibility, forming around them an apparatus of observation, registration and recording, constituting on them a body of knowledge that is accumulated and centralized. The general form of an apparatus intended to render individuals docile and useful, by means of precise work upon their bodies, indicated the prison institution, before the law ever defined it as the penalty par excellence" (p. 231).

Translated by *Helen Domachowski* and *Francisco José Magalhães*

Isabel Carlos

Note: The page numbers accompanying all the quotations in this text refer to the American edition of Michel Foucault's work, *Discipline & Punish, The Birth of the Prison,* translated from French by Alan Sheridan, Vintage Books, February 1979.

Prison gates series

Prison watch-towers series

Frank Thiel, Cottbus, 1992
Prison gates series
c- print
175 x 185 cm

Frank Thiel, Berlin-Rummelsburg, Gate 3, *1991*
Prison gates series
c-print
175 x 170 cm

Frank Thiel, Willich I, 1992
Prison gates series
c-print
175 x 201 cm

Frank Thiel, Cologne, Tower 3, *1992*
Prison watch-towers series
c-print
210 x 175 cm

Frank Thiel, Cologne, Tower 2, *1992*
Prison watch-towers series
c-print
210 x 175 cm

Frank Thiel, Cologne, Tower 1, *1992*
Prison watch-towers series
c-print
210 x 175 cm

Frank Thiel, Cologne, Tower 4, *1992*
Prison watch-towers series
c-print
210 x 175 cm

Frank Thiel, Cologne, Tower 5, *1992*
Prison watch-towers series
c-print
210 x 175 cm

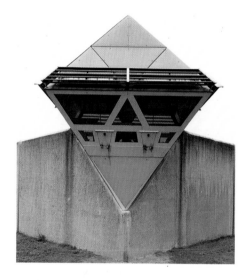

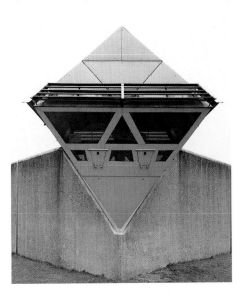  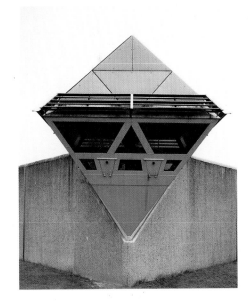

BALTAZAR TORRES

Born 1961, Figueira de Castelo Rodrigo (Portugal)
Lives and works in Portimão (Portugal)

TWO TASTES

In order for us to know how to face the plurality of manifestations within the field of the arts (if there were no other factors of recognition for the artistic fact) Marcel Duchamp's statement would be enough, defining the artist as he who has to create his own language in order to find his own legitimacy.

Baltazar Torres began his career as a sculptor after a brief experience as a painter. And his work has been marked by an incessant (and successful) search for a language of his own, firstly in the several sculptural series; and now in the field of installation.

His sculptures in fact possess an irreducible language which I (for want of better, I admit) have called sculpture-sculpture or sculpture-object. It is a recent tendency, which made his work at the end of the eighties and the beginning of the nineties a proposal in line (or simultaneous) with essentially British currents, although it was not a stylistic "import" or an appropriation of fashion.

This work was characterized by an autonomization of the object in relation to any secure iconographical reference, constructing pure forms which, despite evoking objects from day to day life, also flee from their immediate functionality.

From this point of view I believe that Baltazar Torres' sculptures are "indoor" sculptures, but not only due to their objectual nature. They certainly cannot be used to embellish a corner of a garden or to exalt, for example, a pond. On the contrary, within their minimal scale, they give off intimacy and subjectivity. They are solitary pieces, but of a solitude open to the world, aware of its future, of the slipping by of the days and the hours.

The primeval senses from whence these objects come are the seeing and the looking, minimalizing the real, or autonomizing and objectualizing signs; or even abstracting and minimalizing referents, which are almost always taken from experiences gathered on journeys: they are reduction of urban landscapes, road-scapes, passage-ways (frontiers, tolls, streets, pathways...), of feelings provoked by movement and by the transit of the artist in the world, as if it were a game of lenses and focussings which show an architecture of living experiences, maquettes of the gaze and sceneries of formal passions. It is not by chance, as I will try to prove later on, that Baltazar Torres' recent radical alteration in his work hasn't led him to abandon these creative paradigms...

In the small pieces of sculpture that he produced (Galeria Módulo, 1991), his vocation for the minimal is evident, a vocation which gives rise to a serial treatment. Seriality is one of the key concepts of contemporary art, yet the way that the artist has dealt with it opens the way to an original territory; as such these pieces are contrary to the monumental tendency and the iconographical dependence of a certain (especially Portuguese) sculpture. Baltazar Torres has called seriality into the field of sculpture, creating pieces which function as small isolated realities, but which in their formal exploration (with or without real referents) depict orders, families, genres — in an almost biological strategy. Thus, one of the characteristics of this phase of his work was precisely the ambiguity that such works establish between the organic and the industrial. The chromatic option is a symptom of this, when he used ferrous-green or brown-oxide, bringing out both the porousness and the impurity of the natural world and the instrumentality of the world of machines.

Yet, nothing in this work was the fruit of automatic drawing: the sculptor corrects the pieces, he destroys them and makes them again, he rejects the first configuration, he destabilizes the geometry of the shapes and makes the small traces of iconographical figuration more geometrical.

In the works in wood, (1990, 1991) I believe that there is a greater releasing from figurative (or potentially figurative) elements, and a reinforcing of the pure form. The material established the very facts of the problem: as if it were design without destiny (without designation), like impossible furniture. They are full of formal elegance and seem to summon up a type of "soft" constructivism which planes — even in the literal sense — the harsh right-angles, showing a tendency towards the architectural, as is imposing a glass dome of silence.

Now, the dome of silence has been broken.

The artist, like very few, above all observes and thinks about situations. And he must have suddenly realised the elegant dumbness of his work situated within a world full of noise, of plastic dissentions and unpleasantness.

Baltazar Torres' current work involves — obviously within a continuity in terms of inspiration — a brutal change of scale and an amplification of intentions: where there was minimalism, there is now maximalism; where there was a sort of withheld and reserved beauty (protected from the outside) there is now an evidence of the magnitude of that which surrounds us, as a denouncing; where he was anchored to a poetics "of places" (translated subtlly), our gaze is now attacked by a noisy dysphoria "of sites" (from popular "kitsch" and bourgeois "bad taste"). That is, Baltazar Torres has continued to work within the same field of ideas, but has produced, instead of poetical reductions of the world, amplifications and anamorphoses (sometimes only verifications...) of the unpleasant. The seriality which has always been dear to him is now transposed to a subtle gazing at the contrasts of a country where the First World (the international brands of famous designers which are sold in the shops) and the Third World meet each other; on the other hand the artist doesn't just transpose these realities to the inside of the museum or gallery, but rather continues to work on these referents and amplifies their meaningfulness: the photographs of the houses are placed on the artificial grass carpet, while the names of the brands are subjected to linguistic and phonetical games. Beyond this, the visual clarity and the minimalism of his previous works is projected in these two adjoining rooms of the installation "Produce of..."

The title also forces one to think about the destiny of a small country like Portugal when confronted with binding European directives as a result of its joining the EU. It is obviously not a question of disenchantment. Nor is it a matter of syntonizing the work through channels of socio-political intervention (almost always directed at the mass-media, to its criticism and to an implicit "global art", intimately related to the massification of taste and information). It is, rather, that of showing, in Portugal, what Portugal really has in the field of taste (or bad taste?); without moralizing. And intervening in the visual field, because Baltazar Torres shows us things that everyone can see every day and everywhere. Now they become more visible, which does not mean that they are better or worse. They are certainly the day to day things, by the roadside, in the shop window in the street; they are not sculptural objects, elaborated in the hidden intimacy of a studio: this is the supreme and disconcerting paradox which his work explores, within a critical (and self-critical) dimension.

Translated by *David Alan Prescott*

Isabel Carlos

Baltazar Torres
Installation project-drawing Produce of..., *1994*
Two rooms of 700 x 700 cm each
Installation detail, Venetom-Guimarães, *1994*
Computer-image printed by ink jet

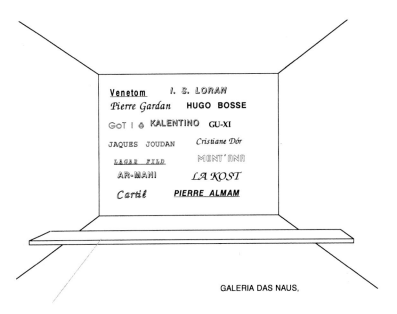

GALERIA DAS NAUS,

Neste suporte, irão ser colocados vários sapatos de homem e senhora com etiquetas das marcas desenhadas na parede

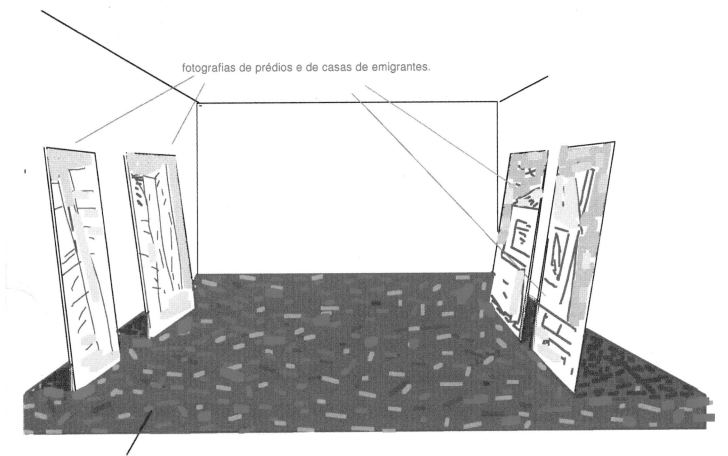

fotografias de prédios e de casas de emigrantes.

Relva artifícial   Galeria das Naus

Baltazar Torres
Sala Vip (Artistas e outros malabaristas)
Weekend News, *installation detail, 1994*
Círculo de Artes Plásticas de Coimbra
Printed paper on cardboard

Baltazar Torres, Respirador, 1991
Iron
21 x 130 x 9 cm

JAMES TURRELL: SELECTED STATEMENTS

The art I do is within this sense of enclosure, I like activating the quality of feeling, living, the sense of territory. It is a fee with which we create the closure ourselves even with a sky that is completely open. We will close it. I like to play with this idea of closure in order to extend our perception in sensing spaces.

One can put semantics and even a sort of priestly personage between you and an experience. This means to achieve this experience one has to pass through such interpretations. It is something that, as a Quaker and even more so as an artist, doesn't interest me. I am not interested in experiences that relate to a brand of religion. This arena of thought has been a concern of art as long as it has existed. For instance, when you enter a cathedral, the experience of the space and light is more likely to engender awe than any rhetoric spoken by the priesthood. Perhaps music comes the closest. For sound has that same directness, which has been the concern of artists and composers for centuries. I choose to be part of this tradition as it cannot be my interest to make things vague. I want a direct experience, to speak about it in a direct language, without any hidden meaning.

During the day, when all things are illuminated, we cannot see the universe. There is no access to the universe, just like when thinking about ourselves we don't see the rest of the world. So having access to the universe very much relies on aspects of the night. It is like having the inside of the house lit at night, then we cannot see the outside. Only when turning the lights out inside, vision and consciousness can move outside. It is about our seeing, about the seeing of ourselves. There is light inhabiting space, light that no longer stays on the wall's surface. What I like most is when we move consciousness and we actually plumb these spaces through vision moving into them. The same way we move into the furthest universe, when we see the universe. Perceiving a starry night one expands into it. It can make people feel very small and have agoraphobia. But this surveying out and having a bigger territory is expansive and thrilling. Just as loneliness is not necessary negative!. A lot of my work is about exploring the quality of seeing yourself see. So literally, when you are presented or confronted with a work of mine, it is something for your seeing and about your seeing, not about mine.

I am interested in the directness of seeing that is comparable to a primal quality of light, almost the deer-running-into-the-headlights type of light. For us it would be more like the impulse to stare into a campfire or a fire in the fireplace. It is not not thinking, but it's not thinking in words. This quality that is engendered by not thinking I like very much and depend on. There is no object because perception itself is the object. There is no image because I want no literal references or storytelling, but essentially I want to focus on this quality of seeing.

I'm interested in imaginative vision meeting physical vision, and where you actually have difficulty telling the difference. First ask yourself: when you dream, where does the light come from? There is a light that has clarity as greater than the daylight vision, and a lucidity of color that's beyond how we see color now. It has a fully formed vision, with characters involved and everything else. This is a seeing that is totally present and it's with the eyes closed. I'm interested in the point where this imaginative vision meets the seeing that comes from what we want to think of as outside physical reality, because it has a lot to do with how we create reality, how we function. And a lot of the pieces I do will at times be on the edge of how we think about reality.

My work takes place between physical limits of perception. That is, our ability to see and not see, and the learned limits, which is how we learned to see. Between these two limits is the area in which my work has its play. I'm very interested in the area in which my work has its play. I'm very interested in the limits of perception and working with those limits, that is, with the physical organism, working with the absolute limits of what we can see and what we can't see and where colors and where peripheral vision come into play. Secondly, I'm interested in learned limits. We've learned to perceive very uniquely in this culture, and differently from other cultures; we have prejudiced perception.

The artist creates and limits the universe of possibilities, and within that you're on your own. In that sense it is like any other art. But it does demand a certain deciding to deal with it, which is this art's price of admission. But every art, I feel, has a price of admission, and often many people don't pay it. They end up looking at the work rather than into it.

One of the strongest qualities you perceive in the experience of my work is the one of the nature of time. It is a really different time than some kinds of art have. In some ways it's heightened, but it's not heightened by speeding up the time as much as it is a slight suspension of the time. My art deals with light itself. It´s not the bearer of the revelation, it is the revelation. I make spaces that are not totally unknown to us, they are similar to dreamlike spaces; when you look into them, the rules seem to be different from the rules of the space in which you are standing. A writer can sometimes conjure up such a space, so powerful that events in the room in which you are reading go unnoticed, because you're in the space often entered while driving. After awhile, we realize we haven't been driving, we've been thinking about something, and we hardly remember the route. We drift off to another place, and we're more there than on the road, but somehow we're able to operate. I like those things to coexist, like a daydream: here's this reality, there's that reality. As we move about these spaces, the reality changes, and I like a state that allows us to assemble the reality ourselves.

No illusion exists in my work, because the space doesn't allude to something that it is not. The light draws attention only to what it is. So when you sense surfaces or borders, these are really there. Surfaces have a tangibility and often convey a tactile sense. I think my work is very sensuous and has a quality of physical presence, but it's not the kind of presence that you can substantiate by reaching our with your hand. However, it is the kind of presence you may want to substantiate that way.

My work definitely deals with a physical, tactile presence of light inhabiting a space, nothing other than the presence. So much of what we know has to do with a physical reality that isn't necessarily the result of touching.

I like the physicality of the work even though there is no material present. I think light is as material as anything else. I built it to be physical, but we've come to think of light as not being at all.

By making something out of light, with light filling space, I am concerned with issues of how we perceive. It's not only a reaction to things physical. For me, working with light in large spaces was more a desire to work in greater realms, a desire that art not be limited to the European structure of works on canvas. This is not too different, perhaps, that the need of composers to expand the possibilities for music, which led to the development of the symphony. Although the symphony required a great deal from society and rather large patronage, it is a form that we've allowed to grow and one that's very good. Before the rise of the symphony, music was limited to what could be made with small instruments. The haiku poem has as much power as a symphony. I think that art should not be limited but be allowed its full range and possibility in material, form, and scale.

In working with light, what is really important to me is to create an experience of wordless thought, to make the quality and sensation of light itself something really quite tactile. It has a quality seemingly intangible, yet it is physically felt. Often people reach out to try to touch it. My works are about light in the sense that light is present and there; the work is made of light. It's not about light or a record of it, but it is light. Light is not so much something that reveals, as it is itself the revelation.

The work I do does not have to do with science or demonstrations of scientific principles. My work has to do with perception, how we see and how we perceive. Though I use the information and need the help of people in the sciences to calculate positions of celestial events and to solve problems of refraction caused by changes in atmospheric pressure and temperature, for example, my work does not push the boundaries of science. I think artists have a lot more to do with investigating the limits of perception than science does at this time. The basic difference, though, is one of intent. I am more interested in posing questions than in answering them. I also think artists are more practical than scientists in that when they find something that works and is useful, they're quite willing to use it without necessarily knowing why or how it works.

Moving from twilight into night is a time when visual changes occur rapidly. Experiences of weather are amazing. If you're going through a fog, using Instrument Flight Rules (IFR) into the clear, you take off and enter the clouds, and just before you break out on top, there's a moment in which the clouds take on the color of the sky. Or coming down to land at night, for instance, doing an IFR approach, there are really interesting things that happen just as you are about to make out the ground below. The experience of flying in snow is another thing; it's a dangerous situation but still very beautiful. Early on I was struck by Antoine de Saint-Exupery's description of flight spaces in his books *Wind, Sand and Stars* and *Night Flight*. He describes spaces in the skies, spaces within space, not necessarily delineated by cloud formation or storms or things like that, but by light qualities, by seeing, and by the nature of the air in certain areas. For me, flying really dealt with these spaces delineated by air conditions, by visual penetration, by sky condition; some were visual, some were only felt. These are the kinds of spaces delineated by air conditions, by visual penetration, by sky conditions; some were visual, some were only felt. These are the kinds of spaces I wanted to work with, very large amounts of space, dealing with as few physical materials as I could .

The sites I like to use are ones that, in general, have no function, spaces that are really only inhabited by consciousness. This inhabiting of space by consciousness is the entry of self into space through the penetration of vision, which is not limited to just that received by the eyes but also has to do with the entry of self into that which is "seen". A lot of spaces are interesting to me when they're generated not by the architecture of form but by the overlay of thought. I'm also interested in public places that are devoid of their function, Mayan and Egypyian ruins, for example, and places such as Mesa Verde. These civilizations adapted natural amphitheaters by building within them to create civic spaces. The fact that they are places of ceremony and ritual and are themselves physically powerful makes them meaningful. The impact of the space of the Gothic cathedral, for example, and the light within it is much more interesting to me than the rhetoric that is spoken there.

Light is a powerful substance. We have a primal connection to it. But, for something so powerful, situations for its felt presence are fragile. I form it as much as the material allows. I like to work with it so that you feel it physically, so you feel the presence of light inhabiting a space. I like the quality of feeling that is felt not only with the eyes. It's always a little bit suspect to look at something really beautiful like an experience in nature and want to make it into art. My desire is to set up a situation to which I take you and let you see. It becomes your experience. I am doing that at Roden Crater. It's not taking from nature as much as placing you in contact with it.

My work is about space and the light that inhabits it. It is about how you confront that space and plumb it. It is about your seeing. How you come to it is important. The qualities of the space must be seen, and the architecture of the form must not be dominant. I am really interested in the qualities of one space sensing another. It is like looking at someone looking. Objectivity is gained by being once removed. As you plumb a space with vision, it is possible to "see yourself see". This seeing, this plumbing, imbues space with consciousness. By how you decide to see it and where you are in relation to it, you create its reality. The piece can change as you move to it or within it. It can also change as the light source that enter it changes.

Roden Crater is a volcanic crater located in an area of exposed geology, the Painted Desert, an area of where you feel geologic time. You have a strong feeling of standing on the surface of the planet. Within that setting, I am making spaces that will engage celestial events. Several spaces will be sensitive to starlight and will be literally empowered by the light of stars millions of light years away. The gathered starlight will inhabit that space, and you will be able to feel the physical presence of that light.

You can inhabit a space with consciousness without physically entering it, as in a dream. You can be in it physically and see it in that manner also. But whether you're in a space and looking at it outside and looking into it, it still has qualities of atmosphere, density, and grain so that your vision will penetrate defferently in some areas than others. Some areas will be more translucent or more opaque, and other areas will be very free to the penetration of vision.

In making a piece, the first objective is not to look at the possibilities of architectural form and the possibilities of space, but to work with them so as to express a particular realm or atmosphere. That's usually done by working with the manner in which the space yields to vision, the way you can plumb the space with seeing like the wordless thought that comes from looking into fire.

Whether or not I want to work with the light that's given depends upon its possibilities of empowering a space. It must have some grace. If not, then I'll use any other light available to me. But it doesn't really matter, because either way the light is used to make a realm that's of the mind.

Daydream spaces, such as those generated by reading a good book, are often more commanding than physical space. While you read, you don't even notice people who walk through the room because you are actually in the space that's generated by the author. This is also true with sound, particularly since the advent of high fidelity and stereophonic sound, the spaces generated by music can be much larger than the one in which you are physically, whether you're in a small room or outside in an open space. This sort of overlay and creation of space that's generated by consciousness is very interesting to me. Another example is when you are driving down a freeway and you find that even though you have been driving reasonably well, you may have missed an exit or in some way feel you haven't really been driving. You've actually been somewhere else, whether it's in deep thought or in the sort of daydream that we often inhabit. This is, I think, the space that we inhabit most of the time, much more than this conscious awake space that is called reality. It's this daydream space overlaid on the conscious awake reality that I like to work with. I'm interested in doing works that seem to come from those places. When you confront a work, you can have knowledge of it already. That is, even though you haven't seen light looking like this or space that is inhabited with light in this manner, it seems to be familiar and comes from a place that you know about.

I'm interested in having a work confront you where you wouldn't ordinarily see it. When you have an experience like that in otherwise normal surrondings, it takes on the lucidity of a dream. The realm of the experience exists between the learned limits of our cultural perception and our physical limits. Because the work exists between those two limits, it has something to do with how we form reality. Though the work is a product of my seeing, it works directly with how you see, as well.

Flying out of South-East Asia over Tibet and amongst the Himalayas, I saw great mountains, jungle and beautiful terrain on journeys that exanded the territories of self. As the instrument of flight becomes more refined, we begin to intellectualize the process and subvert the experience, so that pilots judge each other by their abilities in instrument flight (flight without seeing outside the plane) and in the quality of landing, which is no more than the termination of the experience. It is like judging the dream by the manner in which you awakened. The more you have extraordinary experience in flight, the more you realize the difficulty in passing on the experience to others. Your experience becomes such that it is almost too difficult to talk about it. It seems useless to try to transmit the experience. It would be easier to send others on the flight itself. The idea of the Boddhisattva, one who comes back and entices others on the journey, is to some degree the task of the artist. It is a different role from that of one who is there when you get there. The Boddhisattva entices you to enter that passage, to take the journey. This is where I began to appreciate an art that could be a non-vicarious act, a seeing whose subject was your seeing.

Instead of symbolizing the relationship between the physical plane and those beyond, I wanted a visual confrontation between physical seeing and spaces that created an experience of seeing, familiar to us beyond our conscious awake state, only we had never experienced it that way. This would be a seeing where the space of the sky would be brought into contact with tha space we were in. The sky would no longer be out there, away from us, but in close contact. This plumbing of visual space through the conscious act of moving feeling out through the eyes, became analogous to a physical journey of self as a flight of soul through the planes.

Volcanoes and islands have a terresrial thingness to them. Likewise, my interest in the perception of light is in giving it thingness. It exists just as a physical object has presence. I make thingness of perception by putting limits on it in a formal manner. There is no object there, only objectified perception. By putting into question physicality and objectness, the work may reveal more about physicality than any physical object.

Julia Brown Turrell (Ed.)

James Turrell, Work-draft for the Lisbon installation, 1993

Roden Crater, Flagstaff, Arizona

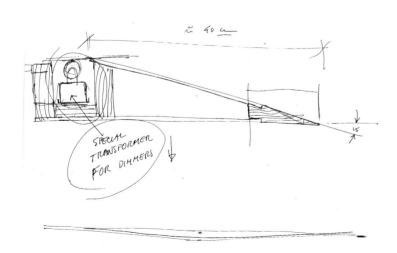

James Turrell, Space That Sees, 1992
The Israel Museum, Jerusalem
Courtesy The Israel Museum, Jerusalem

James Turrell, Gasworks, 1993
The Henry Moore Sculpture Trust, Halifax, England
Courtesy The Henry Moore Sculpture Trust

INFERNAL PARADISE

But I'm not a sculptor. I am a painter who uses long colours.

Xana [1]

This statement by Xana at the beginning of his career (1984), contains the clear-sightedness of first, simple and direct things, and even today, precisely a decade later, still comprises the artist's universe and his stance in relation to art.

First of all, there is a game within the limits of the practices and the disciplines: between painting and sculpture, between design and architecture (Galeria Valentim de Carvalho, February 1990) and, in more recent experiences, between the installation and the individualized objectual investment *Quatro Esculturas* (*Four Sculptures*), Cidade Universitária, Festas de Lisboa, 1991, *Super Plástica*, Galeria Valentim de Carvalho, Lisbon 1993, and also, in the same year, the work *Amor Trabalho Sabedoria* (*Love Work Wisdom*), presented at the Jornadas de Arte Contemporânea of Oporto.

This game is then continued in formal terms and in content: they are objects or canvasses which depict realities, situated between the animal or vegetable kingdom and the artistic universe restricted to the investigation of forms, between wholly created objects (circular structures with bolts and decorative patterns) and day-to-day functional objects (plastic baskets and bath-tubs). There is a term which is constantly (and precisely) evoked when faced with Xana's work: play. This term reveals the dimension of the game which is present throughout Xana's work: "Rarely is a work so affirmatively located within demolished frontiers: painting and sculpture, the popular or childish and the erudite, enjoyment and bewilderment, the immediate intensity of a relationship of fun and the dense charge of meanings and references"[2].

One of the most interesting aspects of work like that of Xana's lies in the way in which it has appropriated itself, transferring the inheritance of Pop to other supports and imaginaries. That is, as the artist suggests in a way in these words — "The world is now pop (Matisse/Warhol), all it needs now is to be superpop"[3] — as Xana radicalizes the main issues of Pop Art, which are immediately evident in the treatment of colour, in the constant use of chromatic artificiality, but also in the implicit problematizing of his works, which are constructed starting from a banalization — now not particularly of the consumer products themselves — but of the very forms and the contemporary experiences.

The artist's objects avoid rigid and cold geometrics or ideal and transcendent configurations, and possess an appropriable dimension, a supremacy of morphology over meaning; they are receptive pieces which arouse the complicity of the gaze, a fruition of the visual more than interrogations or metaphysical perplexities. They are simultaneously a pure exercise in interiority and sensuality: they have nothing pedantic, they do not wish to state any grand idea or theory, to confirm or oppose a tendency. They are close to a certain automatism of the pleasure of drawing or tracing them, they have no intertextuality, they have their own value, and they are autonomized from aesthetic discourse: our gaze is held on his works without the need for decodification, they are there to be seen in the "first degree", they are what they are, in a total effect of selfhood.

This value of selfhood may be one of the factors towards the success and efficiency which Xana's work has received in terms of public showings. In fact, his installations both in the University Campus and in the Metro (1992) demonstrated a powerful capacity to intervene in the urban landscape, in the first case, and in the overloaded urban living-space — an access corridor to the Metro — in the second case. And they turned him into one of the most interesting Portuguese artists, and one of the most gifted for urban art, an area which, after the breaking with modernism, has become one of the most difficult to work in using contemporary languages. There are few artists who, working between the rejection of monumentalism and an eminently abstract discourse, are able to create works for public spaces which are simultaneously of artistic worth and have an urban-communicational value.

Perhaps this is also due to the fact that his works always have the body as something near, in the sense that they establish almost corporal sensations or are even coverings for the body, like the passage-tunnel in *Amor Trabalho Sabedoria* (*Love Work Wisdom*). But always dislocated coverings, inside out, reinforcing the physical and epidermical sensation (the sharp bolts which make it impossible to lean against the walls) or taking this line of work to the limit, operating with the idea of the Home.

In the presentation of the work *Home Sweet Home*, Xana writes: "I start from the search for the ideal space (perfect, Utopian space), towards the creation of a real space, which has this idea as a reference point, here materialized as a house, as the nuclear space of society./ This house is a space where living experiences are accumulated, where we find utilitarian objects, photographic images, or 'constructed objects'. These diverse objects are displayed on a mesh which forces us to feel the space as an all-enveloping whole, like a shell, like a home./ And if I dream of the invention of 'paradise', I might get nearer to 'Hell'".

"Space as an all-enveloping agent": what can be deduced from this is the necessity to create a type of parallel world to the day-to-day world, not really another world, but a world which looks at the same things and uses them with a different way of seeing; to create other landscapes and other objects for the body. The concern with providing a plastic investment for everyday experience and everyday space: "When I do an exhibition it is always a essay on how I would like the world to be"[4].

On the other hand, in this *Home Sweet Home* we find almost a type of self-portrait or self-representation of the artist. In this living-room, bedroom and studio, we notice not only a completely reworked interior according to Xana's image and similarity, but also with references and returnings to previous works, an interior "ideal world" made from the interior of the work itself. And if there is something that Xana managed to achieve long ago, it is a authorial dimension: to establish his own vocabulary and grammar, not to be confused with that of anyone else, which make his works immediately recognizable in terms of authorship.

Xana's work clearly pursues a desire: that of being shared by a great number of people. This is where its radically open character comes from, its lack of theoretical pirouettes, its pleasure in the game and in the colour. Innocent objects which seek out the surface of emotions, which play plasticly with the images that make up our daily lives, essays for a world which seeks out paradise. But probably today the world, even when reduced to the size of the home and to the domestic context, cannot be anything else than an infernal paradise.

[1] Interview to Alexandre Melo and João Pinharanda, "A vida em viewmaster", *Jornal de Letras*, 24/07/84.

[2] Pomar, Alexandre, *Expresso-Revista*, 26/10785 (p. 5R).

[3] IInterview to Luísa Soares de Oliveira, "O mundo já é superpop", *Público*, 9/03/93 (p. 24).

[4] *Op. cit.*

Translated by *David Alan Prescott*

Isabel Carlos

Xana, Home Sweet Home *(installation detail),* 1994
Acrylic on MDF, collages, several furniture,
plastic utensils, waters, various
Three rooms 700 x 700 cm each;
corridor 300 x 2600 cm (approximately)
Sponsored by Plastidom, Câmara Municipal de Lagos,
Artebruta

Xana, Super Plástica, *1993*
Installation
Galeria Valentim de Carvalho, Lisbon
Plastics, acrylic painting on canvas, wood,
painted silk-screen

Xana, Amor, Trabalho, Sabedoria, 1993
Caves da Alfândega do Porto — Installation
Jornadas de Arte Contemporânea do Porto
Wood, buckets, plastic flowers and bathtubs,
water and earth
530 x 500 x 2350 cm

TERREIRO DO PAÇO

In collaboration with

GOETHE-
INSTITUT LISSABON
INSTITUTO ALEMÃO

When, in October 1992, I took charge of the Goethe-Institut of Lisbon, I began by visiting the administrators of the several areas of the organization of Lisbon 94 — European Capital of Culture. During the first conversation with the administrator of the area of exhibitions, Simonetta Luz Afonso, I was asked immediately what project I would suggest for a city like Lisbon. Although at the time I did not know the energetic lady responsible for Portugal's museums, I had imagined that this question might be asked of me and had already thought of an answer: a three-dimensional area of sculptures, in which the works not only correspond with the city, but also with each other. Water, as an element, should also be assimilated within the place for establishing the installation. Simonetta Luz Afonso was greatly enthusiastic about the idea, as the project would have a great impact, which was the aim of the organizers of Lisbon 94. I mentioned a series of European and American *curators*, who had had similar ideas in other cities, and for whom the Lisbon project would represent a special challenge. It would have been necessary for Lisbon 94 to have spent a large part of its finances on the organization of this project, and it would have needed the help of other European countries. But the priorities of Lisbon 94 were others, and the other European countries were not interested. Thus this great dream was not able to be realized in the manner it was initially imagined.

Fortunately it was possible to include the German contribution within the important exhibition, and within the initial aims, *Depois de Amanhã* (*The Day After Tomorrow*).

The Praça do Comércio was already, in my original plan, the heart of the whole project, as it is the focal point of the city, where the principal axis and its hills converge. From the hills, the observer's gaze is directed to beyond the square to the water, and is lost on the water in the distance — the concept of Lisbon 94, which is precisely in accentuating the role of the city as a gateway to Africa and America.

Thus I invited Marie-Jo Lafontaine from Brussels, a teacher in Germany, and the Germans Stephan Balkenhol and Ulrich Horndash in order to, at the invitation of the Goethe-Institut, work on the carrying out of this project which would be the main German contribution to Lisbon 94.

Helmut Friedel's exhibit, like the project, has been changing over the last year and a half. Ulrich Horndash has withdrawn, and Olaf Metzel has joined the project. Marie-Jo Lafontaine's video on the sea and sky of Portugal is to be shown in the Centro Cultural de Belém.

Hans Winterberg

Director of the Goethe-Institut of Lisbon

LISBON '94 — THE GERMAN CONTRIBUTION TO THE EUROPEAN CAPITAL OF CULTURE

OLAF METZEL AND STEPHAN BALKENHOL

Dealing with historical places, with unknown territories, especially when they are places with a strong cultural, political and historical tradition, demands of us the highest degree of respect today. This means that we have to bear a series of considerations in mind so that tones that ring false might not be heard.

What stands out in the urban situation of Lisbon is marked by the Praça do Comércio. This square links the complex network of city streets with the great wide world over the Tagus. Coming from a narrow street, a triumphal arch opens onto a square occupied by a statue of a horseman which imperially gestures towards steps leading to the water. A setting of the like can only be found in Venice, a city whose destinies and history are equally linked to navigation. All of the German works of reflexion for Lisbon 94 — European Capital of Culture are concentrated within this urban situation. Some of the projects planned had to be abandoned when they were seen to be impracticable. There is no doubt that Ulrich Horndash's idea of clearing the square and letting it appear in its original form is fascinating. Like many other great European squares, the Praça do Comércio is also full of parked cars, kiosks, shops and stalls, traffic signs etc., often making it difficult to recognise it. The quality, in the strict sense, of these artisticly created historical spaces is difficult to appreciate and sometimes almost impossible even to imagine. The very idea of reconstructing this original urban condition, that is, of creating an open space within the urban structure, is a sign of a great artistic attitude. To be noticed in a situation defined both artisticly and topographically not through yet another sign, but through the elimination of civilization's junk, thus producing a historical and artistic distinction — all this speaks in favour of an extremely respectful treatment of the culture of another period. Unfortunately, our time seems more ready to work in all senses towards an incrustation, adding more and more new elements, than towards a clarification, reduction or simplification. This does not just have to do with fine arts, as with all the planes of our civilized existence. In emptying an area according to a clear plan, thus bringing it back to its historical basis and reducing it to an architectural measure, Ulrich Horndash's intervention surprises us even more, as Horndash is an artist who well knows how to define his world with images. Starting from Piranesi's illustrations of Rome, Horndash, in a large-scale work entitled *Veduta*, deals with the phenomenon of deconstruction of a skyscraper and of other works of technical construction. The inversion of the constructive process in the destruction suggests the idea of an image with a broad scope. Horndash did not intend to overburden the harmonious architecture of this place with his project, but to create a new image through renunciation.

Another contribution imagined for the Praça do Comércio was that of Marie-Jo Lafontaine. The video artist who initially wanted to show her work on a large video screen ended up by reducing this proposal, throughout the project, to a black and isolated spatial sculpture turned in on itself. In a black cube similar to the Kaaba — the most sacred Muslim place — there was going to be the showing of a film about land, sea and air. This presence, which was supposed to be understood only as a negation, ended up being abandoned, not only because there were extreme technical difficulties, but also because of the question posed by the negative occupation of the square by a black cube, which led to doubts about the reason for its being.

The two projects being carried out by Stephan Balkenhol and Olaf Metzel also aim towards a framework which respects the existing situation as much as possible. Stephen Balkenhol searches, within a defined space, for a place which might demand a sculpture. "I think that in an old city which has grown organically and as such already offers so many 'perfect' situations it is extremely difficult to find a place which still allows an addition'' (Balkenhol).

The appropriate situation which he came across and which seemes to be still open was on the old quay steps, where the Praça do Comércio enters the River Tagus. That is where there are two old stone pillars which support two spheres. One of the spheres had disappeared, leaving one of the pillars naked, and without a function. Pillars have an anthropomorphic character. Generally they are formed of a base, a shaft, and a head-piece. So they are vaguely similar to a human being, especially in their proportions. The pillar with the sphere weighing it down resembles a caryatid, a figure which supports something. In the absence of this weight the pillar expresses a completely different quality. Balkenhol then thought of replacing the absent sphere with a head on top of the pillar or perhaps substituting the two spheres with heads — male and female — looking in opposite directions. By means of this relatively small intervention the given situation would be registered, made more clear and reinforced, and through the artist's sculptural work would take on a new life. Thus would be obtained the right mixture of evidence and irritation. This irritation already existed in Balkenhol as he was dealing with only shafts of pillars in which the spheres had the function of a heading. To substitute a missing sphere with a head would then mean to put into practice an anthropomorphism of a given situation.

Olaf Metzel's considerations have a very similar character within the same situation. He concentrates his work on the Arch of the Rua Augusta. This monumental Triumphal Arch which defines the passage from the square into the urban life of the city is crowned by Victory, who offers the crowns of laurels to the heroes at her feet. Coming from the city to the Tagus, the same monument of the arch of triumph has a different crowning. The face of a richly ornamented clock with garlands and wreaths does not have a continuation with the parapet which crowns the arch. It is in this place, in the space between land and water, between the city and the sea, that Olaf Metzel starts his imaginative considerations. The triumphal arch, as an element of separation and connection, must be given a new touch and a new character with cables and tie-ropes which are typical of a maritime city. Being similar to bronze, and with a green patina, these banal everyday objects would be elevated and would become part of the triumphal level of the existing historical architecture. Through the material, the work is associated with existing elements, such as the bronze crowns, with which Glory crowns Genius and personified bravery. But there would also be a reference to the horseback statue of Dom José I in the Praça do Comércio. The arch would take on a new value by means of the weight of the two pairs of ropes which would crown it, installed on top of the balustrade and of the two ''bronze'' cables tied to the ropes hanging from the parapet. By means of this intervention the triumphal arch gains a new appearance, a stronger accentuation of symmetry. But at the same time it is shown that one cannot change the face of a historically defined square, but only dignify the place on a small scale which duly interprets the dimension of the space itself. The soft arching of the hanging tie-ropes may be interpreted as an answer which spreads the curve of the triumphal arch in order to open it to the heavens. The platform of the triumphal arch which, seen from the hills of the city, stands out from the agglomeration of houses, seems like the bridge of a great ship. With Olaf Metzel's sculpture it acquires the character of anchorage, of tying up, and of connection. Seen in a more formal manner, in the case of the artistic elements used, such simple and reduced forms, they give the impression of being a merely ornamental configuration in a conformity with the decoration already existing around the clock on the triumphal arch. The interlacing and the knots on the tie-ropes reinforce the ornamental nature of the sculpture.

Due to the choice of the material, both Stephan Balkenhol and Olaf Metzel's projects do not appear to have been conceived as temporary interventions, as is the case of an exhibition. On the contrary, they seem to have been there forever and will always remain. For the person in the know, and a daily "user" of Lisbon, who often passes by these places, these interventions will provoke a re-thinking on a situation which has been familiar and habitual to them for a long time, but with time has perhaps become banal. Great artistic urban situations have such a strong meaning for the identification of the inhabitants of the city that they deserve greater care, respect and maintenance than is usual. In this sense, the two artistic projects may also contribute to give greater value to the existing situation.

Helmut Friedel

*Stephan Balkenhol, sketch of the plan for
Cais das Colunas, Lisbon, 1994*

Stephan Balkenhol
Tree heads on dolphins, *1993*
Courtesy Akinci Gallery, Amsterdam
Photo: Victor Arnolds

Stephan Balkenhol
Head on dolphin, *Dordrecht, 1993*
Courtesy Akinci Gallery, Amsterdam
Photo: J. Linders

Olaf Metzel

Born 1952, Berlin
Lives and works in Munich

Olaf Metzel, Girlande, 1994
Arco da Rua Augusta's project drawing,
Lisbon, 1994

Olaf Metzel, Sammelstelle, 1992
Hamburger Kunsthalle, Hamburg
Photo: Gorlich / Metzel

In Situ

In Situ

MIGUEL ÂNGELO ROCHA
Imponderable Landscape

GERARDO BURMESTER
Atelier (exterior)

GERARDO BURMESTER
Atelier (interior)
Sponsored by Riopele

WIM DELVOYE
Chantier

WIM DELVOYE
Chantier (detail)

TARO CHIEZO
Installation

TARO CHIEZO
Calf-Engine

JOÃO PAULO FELICIANO
The Big Red Puff Sound Site

NARELLE JUBELIN
Yarning

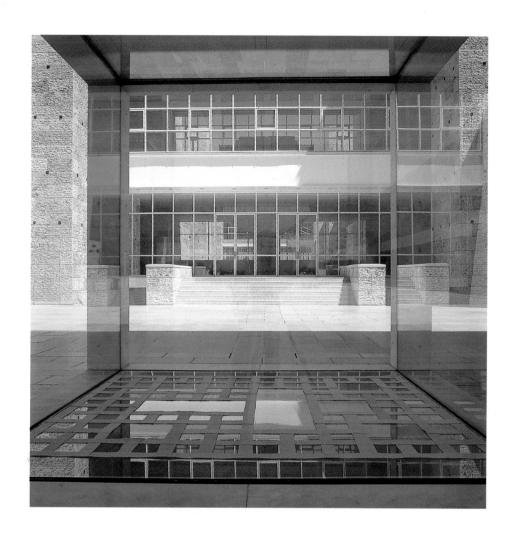

JAMES TURRELL
Installation

Biographies

AUGUSTO ALVES DA SILVA

Born 1963, Lisbon
Lives and works in Lisbon

SOLO EXHIBITIONS

1990   *Algés-Trafaria, 1990* (production Ether / URBE), Ether, Lisbon

1991   *A cidade dos objectos* (for the Centro Português de Design), Fundação de Serralves, Oporto

GROUP EXHIBITIONS (SELECTION)

1991   *Portugal 1890-1990*, Europalia 91 — Portugal, Provinciaal Museum voor Fotografie, Antwerp

1992   *Olho por Olho, uma história de fotografia em Portugal 1839-1992*, Ether, Lisbon

       Une si jolie famille, Le Botanique, Brussels

       Biennale des jeunes createurs 92, Valencia

1994   *Depois de Amanhã / The Day After Tomorrow*, Lisboa 94, Centro Cultural de Belém, Lisbon

---

STEPHAN BALKENHOL

Born 1957, Fritular
Lives and works in Karlsruhe and Meisenthal

SOLO EXHIBITIONS

1984   Galerie Löhrl, Mönchengladbach

1985   A. O. Kunstraum, Hamburg

       Kunstverein Bochum

1987   Kunstverein Braunschweig

       Deweer Art Gallery, Otegem

1988   Galerie Löhrl, Mönchengladbach

       Portikus, Frankfurt

       Kunsthalle, Basel

1989   Kunsthalle, Nuremberg

       Galerie Rüdiger Schöttle, Munich

       Galerie Mai 36, Lucerne

       Galerie Johnen & Schöttle, Cologne

1990   Deweer Art Gallery, Otegem

1991   Galerie Rüdiger Schöttle, Paris

       Skulpturen im Städelgarten, Städtische Galerie im Städel, Frankfurt a. M.

       Galerie Johnen & Schöttle, Cologne

       Kunstverein Ulm

       Galerie Löhrl, Mönchengladbach

       Irish Museum of Modern Art, Dublin

1992   Hamburger Kunsthalle, Hamburg

       Stephan Balkenhol — Kopfe, Kunstverein Maunheim

       Galerie Roger Pailhas, Paris

       Galerie Roger Pailhas, Marseille

       Witte de With, Center for Contemporary Art, Rotterdam

1993   Kabinett für aktuelle Kunst, Bremechaven

       Hirshhorn Museum, Washington

       Stuart Regen Gallery, Los Angeles

       Galerie Johnen & Schöttle, Cologne

       Kunsthalle Karlsruhe

       Deweer Art Gallery, Otegem

1994   Galerie Löhrl, Mönchengladbach

       Kunstraum Neue Kunst, Hanover

Galerie Akinci, Amsterdam

Chateau Rochechouarr, Limoges; Musée des Beaux Arts, Dole; FRAC

Hante-Normandie, Ronen

GROUP EXHIBITIONS (SELECTION)

1990   *A New Necessity*, First Tyne International, Newcastle (Great Britain)

Possible Worlds, Sculpture from Europe, Serpentine Gallery/ICA, London

1991   *7 Women*, Andrea Rosen Gallery, New York

Galerie Rüdiger Schöttler, Munich

Ansichten von Figuren in der Moderne, Stadtisches Museum, Heibronn

10 Jahre Jungen Kunst in Hamburg, Kunstmuseum, Malmö

1992   *Doubletake, Collective Memory &Current Art*, Hayward Gallery and South Bank Centre,

London; Kunsthalle Wien, Vienna

Expo '92, Seville

Double Identity, Galerie Johnen & Schöttle, Cologne

Qui, quoi, où? Un regard sur l'art en Allemagne en 1992, Musée d'Art Moderne de la

Ville de Paris, Paris

Dar gefrorene Leopard Teil III, Galerie Bernd Klüser, Munich

1993   *Kalkhaven*, Dordrecht (Holland)

Gogenbilder, Münster / Westfalen

Kinder, Galerie Rüdiger Schöttle, Munich

1994   Szenenwechsel VI, Museum für Moderne Kunst, Frankfurt a. M.

Depois de Amanhã / The Day After Tomorrow, Lisboa 94, Centro Cultural de Belém, Lisbon

---

GERARDO BURMESTER

Born 1953, Oporto
Lives and works in Oporto

SOLO EXHIBITIONS

1979   *Rupturas*, Fundação Eng.º António de Almeida, Oporto

1980   *Paisagens*, Galeria Diário de Notícias, Lisbon; Fundação Eng.º António de Almeida, Oporto

1981   *O Império do Aborrecimento*, Galeria Roma e Pavia, Oporto

1982   *Mitos Portugueses*, Cooperativa Árvore, Oporto

Pintores, Galeria Roma e Pavia, Oporto

1984   *Portugal é um país bem porreirinho* (installation), Galeria Leo, Lisbon;

Espaço Lusitano, Oporto; Galerie Diagonal, Paris

1988   *1985-1987*, Cooperativa Árvore, Oporto

1989   *Transmutações*, Galeria Roma e Pavia, Oporto

Gleich und Gleich, Galeria Diferença, Lisbon

Reencontro, Galeria Alda Cortez, Lisbon

1990   *Reencontro II*, Galeria Pedro Oliveira, Oporto

1991   *Amadeo*, Museu Municipal Amadeo de Sousa-Cardoso, Amarante (Portugal)

1992   *Arquipélagos Vermelhos*, Galeria Pedro Oliveira, Oporto

1993   *Contaminações*, Galeria Pedro Oliveira, Oporto

1994   *Registos*, Galeria Alda Cortez, Lisbon

GROUP EXHIBITIONS (SELECTION)

1990   *Cabrita Reis, Gerardo Burmester, Nancy Dwyer, Stephan Huber*, Galeria Pedro Oliveira, Oporto

1991   *Tríptico*, Europalia 91 — Portugal, Museum van Hedendaagse Kunst, Gent

Há um minuto do mundo que passa — obras na Colecção da Fundação de Serralves,

Fundação de Serralves, Oporto

Contingências, Casa das Artes, Oporto

61 obras de arte, Forum, Maia (Portugal)

1992   *Fundação de Serralves, Um Museu Português*, Seville

       10 Contemporâneos, Fundação de Serralves, Oporto

       Sortilégios, 1.ᵃˢ Jornadas de Arte Contemporânea Porto '92, Alfândega do Oporto

1993   *Tradicion, Vangarda e Modernidade do século XX português*, Auditório de Galicia, Santiago de Compostela

       V Bienal de Escultura e Desenho, Caldas da Rainha (Portugal)

       Colecção da Caixa Geral de Depósitos, Lisbon

1994   3.ᵃ Biennal Martinez Guerricabeita de la Universitat de Valencia, — Palau dels Scala, Valencia

       Depois de Amanhã / The Day After Tomorrow, Lisboa 94, Centro Cultural de Belém, Lisbon

PERFORMANCES

1976   III Encontros Internacionais de Arte, Póvoa de Varzim (Portugal)

1977   *Grupo Puzzle*, IV Encontros Internacionais de Arte em Portugal, Caldas da Rainha (Portugal)

       Grupo Puzzle, Identidade Cultural, Massificação, Originalidade, SNBA, Lisbon

1978   *Grupo Puzzle, Peinture Portugaise Actuelle*, Prétigny (France)

       Grupo Puzzle, 29éme Salon de la jeune peinture, Paris

1979   *Grupo Puzzle*, Fundação Eng.º António de Almeida, Oporto

       Grupo Puzzle, Puzzle convida ex-puzzles, Sindicato dos Seguros do Norte, Oporto

       Grupo Puzzle, performance at the Toulouse Le Mirail University, Toulouse

       Grupo Puzzle, I Symposium Internacional de Arte da Performance, Lyon

1982   Galerie J. J. Donguy, Paris

       Encontros de Performance, Nice; Galerie Pali-Kao, Paris

1983   Festival de Performance do Espaço Lusitano, Oporto

1984   Centre Georges Pompidou, Paris

1985   *Art is action*, Kassel

       Perfo-3, Rotterdam

1986   I Encontro Nacional de Performance, Torres Vedras (Portugal)

1987   *Performance arte*, Fundação Calouste Gulbenkian, Lisbon

       Festival Internacional de Performance, Oporto

COLLECTIONS

Museu de Amarante (Amarante); Fundação de Serralves (Oporto); Banco Português do Atlântico (Oporto); Caixa Geral de Depósitos (Lisbon); Fundação Eng.º António de Almeida (Oporto).

PEDRO CABRITA REIS

Born 1956, Lisbon
Lives and works in Lisbon

SOLO EXHIBITIONS

1981   *25 Desenhos*, SNBA, Lisbon

       Até ao regresso, Galeria Diferença, Lisbon

1983   *Pinturas*, SNBA, Lisbon

       Cenas da Caça e da Guerra, Galeria Diferença, Lisbon

1984   *Os discretos mensageiros*, Galeria Cómicos, Lisbon

1985   *De um santuário e certos lugares*, Galeria Jornal de Notícias, Oporto

1986   *Da Ordem e do Caos*, Galeria Cómicos, Lisbon

1987   *Anima et macula*, Galerie Cintrik, Antwerp

       Cabeças, Árvores e Casas, Galeria Roma e Pavia, Oporto

1988   *A sombra na água*, Galeria Cómicos, Lisbon

1989   *Melancolia*, Bess Cutler Gallery, New York

1990   *A casa dos suaves odores*, Galeria Cómicos / Luís Serpa, Lisbon

        Alexandria, Convento de S. Francisco, Beja (Portugal)

        A casa da paixão e do pensamento, Galeria Juana de Aizpuru, Madrid

        A casa da ordem interior, Galerie Joost Declerq, Gent (Belgium)

        Silêncio e Vertigem, Igreja de Santa Clara-a-Velha, Coimbra (Portugal)

        Cabrita Reis: Sculpture, Barbara Farber Gallery, Amsterdam

1991   *Vite Parallele*, Sala Umberto Boccioni, Milan

        Os lugares cegos, Galerie Jennifer Flay, Paris

        Pedro Cabrita Reis, Rhona Hoffman Gallery, Chicago

        Pedro Cabrita Reis, Burnett Miller Gallery, Los Angeles

        A cidade levantada, Galeria Juana de Aizpuru, Seville

1992   *Uma Luz Interdita*, Kunstraum München, Munich

1993   *H. Suite (piezas de Madrid)*, Galeria Juana de Aizpuru, Madrid

        Uber Malerei, Galerie Ludwig, Krefeld

1994   *Echo der Welt*, Mala Galerija, Ljubljana

        A Sala dos Mapas, Museu José Malhoa, Caldas da Rainha (Portugal)

        Contra a Claridade, CAM-JAP / Fundação Calouste Gulbenkian, Lisbon

GROUP EXHIBITIONS (SELECTION)

1990   *Ultima Frontera: 7 artistes portuguesos*, Centro de Arte Santa Monica, Barcelona

        Cabrita Reis, Rui Sanches, Fundación Luis Cernuda, Seville

        Ponton-Temse, Temse (Belgium)

        Carnets de Voyage I, Fondation Cartier, Jouy-en-Josas

1991   *Metropolis*, Martin-Gropius-Bau, Berlin

        Tríptico, Europalia 91 — Portugal, Museum van Hedendaagse, Gent (Belgium)

1992   *Los ultimos dias*, Salas del Arenal, Seville

        Tisina, Prostislovne Oblike Resnice / Silence, Contradictory shapes of truth, Moderna Galerija, Ljubljana

        Documenta IX, Kassel

        Silence to Light, The Watari Museum of Contemporary Art, Tokyo

1993   *Douze Oeuvres dans l'Espace*, Centre d'Art Contemporain Domaine de Kerguehennec (France)

        De la main à la Tête, l'objet théorique, Centre d'Art Contemporain Domaine de Kerguehennec (France)

        Nos rêves façonnent le Monde, Cimaise et Portique Moulins Albigeois, Albi

        Jimmie Durham, David Hammons, Pedro Cabrita Reis, Friart, Centre d'Art Contemporain, Friburg

        Western Lines, Hara Museum, ARC, Gunma (Japan)

        Cerco — BIO 93, Óbidos (Portugal)

        Camaras de Friccion, Galeria Luis Adelantado, Valencia

1994   *Depois de Amanhã / The Day After Tomorrow*, Lisboa 94, Centro Cultural de Belém, Lisbon

PEDRO CALAPEZ

Born 1953, Lisbon
Lives and works in Lisbon

SOLO EXHIBITIONS

1989   *Grafites*, Galeria Alda Cortez, Lisbon

       Desenhos sobre Madeira, CAM / Fundação Calouste Gulbenkian, Lisbon

1990   *Passagens*, installation in Convento de S. Francisco, Beja (Portugal)

       As Ruínas Circulares, Galeria Atlântica, Oporto

1991   *Estranhas Figuras*, installation in (Convento dos Capuchos), Portugal

       Histórias de Objectos, Casa de la Cittá, Roma; Carré des Arts, Paris;

       Fundação Calouste Gulbenkian, Lisbon

       Desenhos de Objectos, Galerie Florence Arnaud, Paris

       Trabalhos sobre Papel, Galeria Diferença, Lisbon

1992   *12 Pedaços*, Galeria Trem, Faro (Portugal)

       ramos cérebros-folhas tubagens-circuitos, Galeria Cómicos / Luís Serpa, Lisbon

1993   *Petit jardin et paysage*, installation in Chapelle la Salpêtriére, Paris

       Cidades contínuas, Paço Imperial, Rio de Janeiro and Centro Cultural de S. Paulo

GROUP EXHIBITIONS (SELECTION)

1991   *A secreta vida das imagens*, Galeria Atlântica, Lisbon

       21.ª Bienal de S. Paulo

1992   *Nova pintura e nova escultura portuguesa*, Casa Garden, Macau

       4 artistas portugueses, Ho Gallery, Hong Kong

       10 Contemporâneos, Casa de Serralves, Oporto

       Arte Contemporânea Portuguesa na Colecção da Fundação Luso-Americana

       para o Desenvolvimento, CAM / Fundação Calouste Gulbenkian, Lisbon

1994   *Depois de Amanhã / The Day After Tomorrow*, Lisboa 94, Centro Cultural de Belém, Lisbon

SHOWS

1987   *Le Travail du Peintre* (with Nuno Vieira de Almeida), Acarte, CAM / Fundação Calouste

       Gulbenkian, Lisbon

1989   *A Viagem de Inverno*, Acarte, CAM / Fundação Calouste Gulbenkian, Lisbon

1993   *Zerlina*, set design for the Teatro Nacional Dona Maria II, Lisbon

COLLECTIONS

Museu Nacional de Arte Moderna (Oporto); Secretaria de Estado da Cultura (Lisbon); Fundação

Calouste Gulbenkian (Lisbon); Fundação Luso-Americana para o Desenvolvimento (Lisbon);

Ministério das Finanças (Lisbon); Banco de Portugal (Lisbon); Caixa Geral de Depósitos (Lisbon);

Chase Manhattan Bank NA (New York).

TARO CHIEZO

Born 1962, Tokyo
Lives and works in Tokyo and New York

SOLO EXHIBITIONS

1992   Shiraishi Contemporary Art Inc., Tokyo

Mars Gallery, Tokyo

1993   Sandra Gering Gallery, New York

Gallery Cellar, Nagoya

GROUP EXHIBITIONS (SELECTION)

1991   *Invisible Body*. Curated by Alan Jones, Rempire Gallery, New York

Hotel 48 hrs. Off-Soho suites, New York

Universe in The Box, Tierrart Gallery, Tokyo

The Booth Show. Curated by Alan Jones, Mini Mall at Soho, New York

1992   *Post Human*. Curated by Jeffrey Deitch,

FAE Musée D'Art Contemporain, Lausanne

Castello di Rivoli, Museo D'Arte Contemporanea, Turin

Deste Foundation for Contemporary Art, Athens

Deichtorhallen, Hamburg

Summer Becomes Eclectic, Mars Gallery, Tokyo

1993   *Slittamenti*. Curated by Christian Leigh

Zitelle, Biennale Venezia, Italy

Annina Nosei Gallery, New York

Bodyguard, Hohenthal und Bergen, Munich

New Self. Curated by Jeffrey Deitch

Nanba City Hall, Osaka

Sound. Curated by Marisa Vescovo

Museion Museo D'Arte Moderna, Italy

Summer Punch'93, Kim Light Gallery, Los Angeles

Hotel 48 Stunden, Modern Hotel Garni, Düsseldorf

1994   *Depois de Amanhã / The Day After Tomorrow*, Lisboa 94, Centro Cultural de Belém, Lisbon

---

JOSÉ PEDRO CROFT

Born 1957, Oporto
Lives and works in Lisbon

SOLO EXHIBITIONS

1983   Galeria Diário de Notícias, Lisbon

1984   Galeria Leo, Lisbon

1985   Galeria Leo, Lisbon

1989   Galeria Diferença, Lisbon

Galeria Atlântica, Oporto

1990   Galeria Athenea, Barcelona

1991   Galeria Alda Cortez, Lisbon

Galeria Atlântica, Lisbon / Oporto

Galeria Alda Cortez (engraving), Lisbon

Ado Gallery, Antwerp

1992   Galeria Valentim de Carvalho, Lisbon

Galeria Berini, Barcelona

Galeria Alda Cortez, Lisbon

1993   Galeria Fucares, Madrid

Galeria Tristan Barbara (engraving), Barcelona

1994 Galeria Alda Cortez, Lisbon

CAM / Fundação Calouste Gulbenkian, Lisbon

GROUP EXHIBITIONS (SELECTION)

1990 *Homenagem a João Cutileiro*, Fundação Calouste Gulbenkian, Lisbon

Ultima Fronteira — 7 artistes portuguesos, Centro de Arte Santa Monica, Barcelona

Galeria Margo Leavin, Los Angeles

Pontom-Temse, Museum van Hedendaagse Kunst, Gent, Temse (Belgium)

1991 *A secreta vida das imagens*, Galeria Atlântica, Lisbon / Oporto

Tríptico, Europalia 91 — Portugal, Museum Van Hedendaagse Kunst, Gent

Há um minuto do mundo que passa, obras na colecção da Fundação de Serralves, Fundação de Serralves, Oporto

1992 *Fundação de Serralves, Um Museu Português*, Seville

Arte Contemporânea Portuguesa na Colecção da Fundação Luso-Americana para o Desenvolvimento, CAM / Fundação Calouste Gulbenkian, Lisbon

10 Contemporâneos, Fundação de Serralves, Oporto

Silence to Light, The Watari Museum of Contemporary Art, Tokyo

1993 *Meeting Points*, Galeria Tomas March, Valencia, Galeria Fucares, Almagro

Exposição da Colecção da FLAD, Museu José Malhoa, Caldas da Rainha (Portugal)

V Bienal Internacional de Escultura e Desenho (invited artist), Caldas da Rainha (Portugal)

Ilegítimos, Jóias Portuguesas Contemporâneas 1993, Artefacto 3, Lisbon

Arte Moderna em Portugal, Colecção de Arte da Caixa Geral de Depósitos, Culturgest Galeria I, Lisbon

Sete Sentidos — sete artistas portugueses na colecção da FLAD, Palau Robert, Barcelona

1994 *Perspectives*, Centre d'Art Contemporain la Ferme du Buisson, Noisiel (France)

Depois de Amanhã / The Day After Tomorrow, Lisboa 94, Centro Cultural de Belém, Lisbon

COLLECTIONS

Centro de Arte Moderna / Fundação Calouste Gulbenkian (Lisbon); Casa de Serralves, (Oporto); Fundação Luso-Americana para o Desenvolvimento (Lisbon); Caixa Geral de Depósitos (Lisbon); Museo Nacional Centro de Arte Reina Sofia (Madrid).

WIM DELVOYE

Born 1965, Wervik (Belgium)
Lives and works in Gent (Belgium)

SOLO EXHIBITIONS (SELECTION)

1986 Galerie Plus-Kern, Brussels

1988 Galerie Riekje Swart, Amsterdam

Galleria Andrea Murnik, Milan

Galerie Plus-Kern, Brussels

1989 Galerie Bébert, Rotterdam

1990 Jack Tilton Gallery, New York

1991 Sonnabend Gallery, New York

Galerie Lehmann-Faust, Geneva

Art Gallery of New-South-Wales, Sydney

Castello di Rivoli, Rivoli, Turin

1992   Kunsthalle Nürnberg, Nürnberg

Galerie Micheline Swajeer, Antwerp

Sonnabend Gallery, New York

Ruth Bloom Gallery, Los Angeles

1993   Galeria Tucci Russo, Turin

Galerie Ghislaine Hussenot, Paris

Galerie Lehmann, Lausanne

1994   Galerie Beaumont, Luxemburg

Center for the Arts, S. Francisco, California

GROUP EXHIBITIONS (SELECTION)

1990   *Avec*, Centre d'Art Contemporain APAC, Nvers

Blau, Farbe der Ferne, Heidelberger

Kunstverein, Heidelberg

Aperto, Biennale di Venezia, Venice

Artists (from Flanders), Palazzo Sagredo, Venice

Zoersel '90, Zoersel

Belgique, une nouvelle Génération, Fonds Régionaux pour l'Art Contemporain de la Loire,

Clisson

Confrontationes, Museo Español de Arte Contemporaneo, Madrid

Kunstenaars (van Vlaanderen), Museum van Hedendaagse Kunst, Gent (Belgium)

1991   *Kunst, Europa, Belgien, Niederlande, Luxemburg*, Kunstverein, Düsseldorf

Anni Novanta, Galleria Comunale d'Arte Moderna; Musei Comunali Rimini

(ex-colonia «Le Navi»), Bologna

Büchstablich, Van der Heydt-Museum, Wuppertal / Kunsthalle Barmen / Wuppertal

Elberfeld

Desplaziamentos, Cientro Atlantico de Arte Moderno, Las Palmas

Altrove, Museo di Arte Contemporanea, Prato

The Belgian Boom, Miami Dade Community College, Miami

1992   *Selectie Belgische Kunstenaars voor*, Documenta IX, Museum Dhondt-Dhaenens, Deurle

Documenta IX, Kassel

The Biennale of Sydney, Sydney

Post-Human, FAE Musée d'Art Contemporain, Pully / Lausanne, Castello di Rivoli, Rivoli,

Turim, e Deste Foundation, Athens

Territorio Italiano, Spazio Opus / Documentario, Milan

Drei Künstler aus Belgien, Salzburger Kunstverein, Salzburg

1993   *Post-Human*, Deichtorhallen, Hamburg; The Israel Museum, Jerusalem

De la main à la tête, l'objet théoretique, Domaine de Kerguehennec, Kerguehennec

Curios and Mirabilia, Château d'Oyron

Good News, Galleria Cardi, Milan

1994   *EV + A Invited*, Limerick

Depois de Amanhã / The Day After Tomorrow, Lisboa 94, Centro Cultural de Belém, Lisbon

JOÃO PAULO FELICIANO

Born 1963, Caldas da Rainha (Portugal)
Lives and works in Lisbon

SOLO EXHIBITIONS

1985   Galeria Alfarroba, Cascais (Portugal)

The Armory Shown, Sociedade Nacional de Belas Artes, Lisbon

Pontes e Passagens de Nível, Galeria Capc, Coimbra (Portugal)

1987   *A Arte da Cura*, Museu de Setúbal, Setúbal (Portugal)

Pinturas e Objectos de Parede, Galeria Capc, Coimbra (Portugal)

1988   Galerie De Equilibrist, Sint-Nicklaas (Belgium)

1989   *Portugal + Feliciano*, Galerie Transit, Louvain

1990   Galeria Graça Fonseca, Lisbon

Galeria Oliva Arauna, Madrid

1993   *I've Always Loved you*, Galeria Graça Fonseca, Lisbon

1994   Mousunturm, Frankfurt

GROUP EXHIBITIONS (SELECTION)

1990   *Accrochage*, Galerie Christine et Isy Brachot, Brussels

Ases da Paleta, Galeria Quadrum, Lisbon

Galerie De Equilibrist, Sint-Nicklaas (Belgium)

Loja de Desenho, Lisbon

Rien ne va plus Faites vos Y(j)eux, H.A.C.K., Den Haag (Holland)

1991   Galeria Graça Fonseca, Lisbon

Tendências, Forum Picoas, Lisbon

The Floor Show, Galerie De Equilibrist, Sint-Nicklaas (Belgium)

Manifesto, Convento de S. Francisco, Beja (Portugal)

1992   *Already Made*, Galeria Graça Fonseca, Lisbon

Reencontros, Galeria Alda Cortez, Lisbon

Finisterra, Circulo de Bellas Artes, Madrid

1993   *Imagens para os anos 90*, Fundação de Serralves, Oporto, and Culturgest, Lisbon

1994   *The Independent Worm Saloon*, Sociedade Nacional de Belas Artes, Lisbon

Múltiplas Dimensões, Centro Cultural de Belém, Lisbon

Uno cada Uno, Galeria Juana de Aizpuru, Madrid

Depois de Amanhã / The Day After Tomorrow, Lisboa 94, Centro Cultural de Belém, Lisbon

LIVE PERFORMANCES

1986/88   Several performances with Café Malevitch

1989/94   Regularly work with Tina & The Top Ten

1990   C.A.M. / Fundação Calouste Gulbenkian, Lisbon (with L. Desirat, J. P. Lorena and J. O. e Silva)

With No Noise Reduction, Johnny Guitar, Lisbon

1991   With Rafael Toral, *Concerto para 10 Guitarras*, Galeria Monumental, Lisbon

1991/92   Around 20 gigs with Pop Dell'Arte

1992   With The Moneyland Experience, Palau de Musica, Valencia

1993   *Automated Guitars*, Aniki Bóbó, Oporto

With Mad Crash: Four Necks, Sintra (Portugal)

iEar Studios, Rensselear Polythecnic Institute, Troy, U.S.A

Experimental Intermedia Foundation, New York (with Roger Kleyer, Annie Gosfield and David T. Dienes)

With No Noise Reduction: performance *Solo For Voice N.º 23 de John Cage*, Galeria Graça Fonseca, Lisbon

1994   Urban Aboriginals Festival, Berlin (with Mimi)

        Bar Europa, Lisbon (with L. Desirat, Ed. Cunha and M. Feliciano)

        Johnny Guitar, Lisbon (with R. Toral, Sei Miguel and Jane Henry)

RECORDING

        With No Noise Reduction:

1991   Participated in the Vítor Rua *Vidia* project

        Em Tempo Real, CD, El Tatu Records, Lisbon

        With Pop Dell'Arte:

1992   Distorção Caleidoscópica, compilation, MTM records, Oporto

        3 x 7" Singles, compilation, Moneyland Records, Lisbon

        2002, Maxi-single, Variadisc, Lisbon

        Ready Made, Variadisc, Lisbon

1993   *Everslick*, 7" Single, Moneyland Records, Lisbon

        With Tina and the Top Ten:

1994   *Teenage Drool*, CD, El Tatu Records

VIDEOS

1993   *Northern Tives*, 2' 30"

        The Pain of Breathing (computer loop on tape)

        Real McKoy Collective Word Video

        Mind Your Own Business

        Crash Music

        Several videos for Tina and the Top Ten and other bands.

ÂNGELA FERREIRA

Born 1958, Maputo
Lives and works in Lisbon

SOLO EXHIBITIONS

1983   University Gallery, Cape Town

1989   Market Gallery, Johannesburg

1990   CAM / Fundação Calouste Gulbenkian, Lisbon

1992   *The Annexe*, South African National Gallery, Cape Town

1993   Galeria Módulo, Lisbon

GROUP EXHIBITIONS (SELECTION)

1991   *Recent Acquisitions*, South African National Gallery, Cape Town

1993   *New Wood Sculptures*, South African National Gallery, Cape Town

1994   *Depois de Amanhã / The Day After Tomorrow*, Lisboa 94, Centro Cultural de Belém, Lisbon

COLECÇÕES

Michaelis School of Fine Art Collection. UCT; Market Gallery Foundation (Johannesburg); Fundação Calouste Gulbenkian (Lisbon); South African National Gallery (Cape Town); The Johannesburg Art Gallery (Johannesburg).

NARELLE JUBELIN

Born 1960, Sydney
Lives and works in Sydney

SOLO EXHIBITIONS

1986   *Remembrance of Things Past Lays Bare the Plans for Destiny*, Avago, Sydney

        His Story, Mori Gallery, Sydney

1987   *Re-presenting His Story*, Institute of Technology, Architecture Faculty Gallery, Sydney

1988   *Second Glance (at the Coming Man)*, College Gallery, Adelaide, and Mori Gallery, Sydney

1989　*Second Glance (at the Coming Man)*, George Paton Gallery, Melbourne, and University of
        Tasmania Gallery, Hobart
1991　*Cloth*, Mori Gallery, Sydney
1992　*Dead Slow*, Centre for Contemporary Art, Glasgow
        Estate, Knoll Galerie, Vienna
1993　*Estate*, Knoll Galeria, Budapest
1994　*Soft Shoulder*, Renaissance Gallery, Chicago

COLLABORATIVE EXHIBITIONS

1985　*Narelle Jubelin / Paul Saint,* Plan Z Gallery, Sydney
1987　*The Crossing*, with Adrienne Gaha, First Draft, Sydney
1993　*Old Love*, with Satoru Itasu, Gallery Lunami, Tokyo

GROUP EXHIBITIONS (SELECTION)

1990　*Trade Delivers People*, in *Aperto*, Venice Biennale, Venice
        Adelaide Biennial, Art Gallery of South Australia, Adelaide
        Paraculture, Artists Space, New York
1991　*Foreign Affairs*, in *Places with a Past: New Site Specific Art in Charleston*, Spoletto Festival, USA
        Frames of Reference: Aspects of Feminism and Art, Pier 4, Sydney
        The Subversive Stitch, Monash University Gallery, Melbourne, and Mori Annexe Sydney
1992　*Molteplici Culture*, Convento di S. Egidio, Rome
        Internal Affairs, in *Working in Public*; in collaboration with Allan Cooley, Philippine Consul
        General and Trade Offices, Sydney
        Doubletake; Collective Memory & Current Art, Hayward Gallery, London and Kunsthalle, Vienna
        The Boundary Rider, Ninth Biennale of Sydney, Bondstore, Sydney
1993　*Looking at Seeing and Reading*, Ivan Dougherty Gallery, Sydney (touring)
        Sshhh..., Mori Gallery, Sydney
1994　*Trade Delivers People; second version*, National Gallery of Victoria, Melbourne
        Depois de Amanhã / The Day After Tomorrow, Lisboa 94, Centro Cultural de Belém, Lisbon

---

MARIE JO LAFONTAINE

Born 1950, Antwerp
Lives and works in Brussels

VIDEOGRAPHY

VIDEO INSTALLATIONS

1979　*La batteuse de Palplanches*
1980　*La marie-salope*
1981　*Round around the ring*
1982　*Le rêve d'Héphaistos*
1983　*His master's voice*
1984　*Attaco!*
　　　A las cinco de la tarde
1985　*Le metronome de Babel*
1985　*Les larmes d'acier*
1986　*L'enterrement de Mozart*
1987/88　*Victoria*
1989/90　*Passio*
1986/91　*Jeux interdits*
1991　*We are all shadows*

1991/92   *Jedel Engel ist Schrecklich*

Video-films

1986   *The Labyrinth of Beauties*

1988   *Portrait volé d'un voyeur portrait de Jean Nouvel - Architect*

Solo exhibitions

1976   Galerie Walter Thompson, Brussels

1977   Galerie Anne van Horenbeek, Brussels

1979   *Monochromes noir*, Palais des Beaux-Arts, Brussels

Galerie Les contemporains, Genval-Lac

La batteuse de palplanches, ICC, Antwerp

1981   *Round around the Ring*, Musée d'Art Moderne / Centre Georges Pompidou, Paris

1982   CAPC, Bordeaux

1983   Maison de la Culture, La Rochelle

Gemeente Museum, Den Haag (Holland)

1984   Musée d'Art Moderne / Centre Georges Pompidou, Paris

Galerie Powerhouse, Montreal

Octobre des Arts, ELAC, Lyon

1985   Maison de la Culture, La Rochelle

Vidéographie, Cirques Divers, Liège

Maison de la Culture, Le Havre

Carpenter Center Havard University, Boston

A las cinco de la tarde, Tate Gallery, London

A las cinco de la tarde et les gardiens du jeux, Musée d'Art Moderne, Villeneuve d'Asq

1986   *Des jeux pour réjouir le regard des Dieux*, Musée Cantini, Marseille

Salle Petrarque, Montpellier

Art jonction International, Nice

A las cinco de la tarde, Sprengel Museum, Hanover

1987   *L'interdit desiré*, Musée de Brou, Bourg-en-Bresse

Gemeente Museum, Arnheim

Gallery de Gryse, Tielt

Centre d'Art Contemporain, Orleans

Koninkelijk Muziekconservatorium, Gent (Belgium)

Galerie Roger Pailhas, Marseille

1988   Museum of Contemporary Art, LACMA, Los Angeles

Museum für Gegenwartskunst, Basel

Galerie Walter Storms, Munich

Galerie Wanda Reiff, Maastricht

Forum with Galerie Walter Storms, Hamburg

1989   Jack Shainmann Gallery, New York

Weisses Haus, Hamburg

Galerie Michael Horbach, Cologne

The Fruitmarket Gallery, Edimburg

Whitechapel Art Gallery, London

1990   *Passio*, Städtisches Museum Abteiberg, Mönchengladbach

A fleur du mal, Salzburger Kunstverein, Salzburg

A fleur du mal, Städtisches Museum Schloss Hardenberg, Velbert

Widerstand, Städtische Galerie, Göppingen

Savoir retenir et fixer ce qui est sublime, Musée des Beaux-Arts, Tourcoing

La vie... une hésitation, Galerie Montaigne, Paris

1991 *L'étoile filante*, Wewerka-Weiss Galerie, Berlin

Ric Urmel Gallery, Gent (Belgium)

Immaculta, Bergkerk Kunst, Deventer

Galerie Walter Storms, Munich

We are all shadows

1992 *Memoria*, Archief, Den Haag (Holland)

Galerie Montaigne, Paris

Vereins und Westbank, Hamburg

Métronome de Babel, Musée Lubeck, Lubeck

And after the orgy, Noordijlaandskunstmuseum, Aalborg

History is against forgiveness, Goethe Institut, Brussels

We are all shadows II, Museum of Art, Foundation Helena Rubinstein, Tel-Aviv

1993 *Als das Kind noch Kind war*, Galerie Bugdahn, Düsseldorf

Himmel und Hölle, Galerie Deweer, Otegem

1994 Guggenheim Museum, New York

victoria, Smith College Museum, Massachusetts

Galeria Cómicos, Lisbon

savoir retenir et fixer ce qui est sublime, University Art Museum California State, Long Beach, California

Wanâs Mobile, Malmö

Galerie Walter Storms, Munich

Jeder Engel ist schrecklich, Gasometer, Oberhausen

GROUP EXHIBITIONS (SELECTION)

1990 *Threshold*, The National Museum of Contemporary Art, Oslo

Zur Sache Selbst, Wiesbaden Museum, Wiesbaden

40 ans de la jeune Peinture Belge, Palais des Beaux Arts, Brussels

Un art de la Distinction, Abbaye Saint André

Centre d'Art Contemporain, Meymac

The Readymade Boomerang, 8th Biennale of Sydney, Sydney

1991 *Sport – Sinn und Wahn*, Palais Freiberger, Mürzzuschlag

Multimediale 2, Zentrum für Kunst und Medientechnologie, Karlsruhe

Et Alia, Galerie Jule Kewenig, Frechem-Bachem

Argusauge, Glyptothèque, Munich

Artec 91, City Museum, Nagoya (Japan)

The Belgian Boom, Centre Gallery University, Miami

1992 *Kunst Videnskab*, Charlottenborg, Copenhagen

Force Sight, Schloss Presteneck, Stein am Kocher

Moving Image, Musée Fundación Miró, Barcelona

Galerie Bugdahn, Düsseldorf

Nouvelle Genération, Galerie Beaumont, Luxemburg

Tradition der Moderne, IG Métal Gewerkschaft, Frankfurt, Stuttgart, Berlin

Word and Image, MUHKA, Antwerp

1993   *Feuer, Wasser, Licht, Erde*, DeichtoorHalle, Hamburg

Deutschsein, Städtische Kunsthalle, Düsseldorf

Flander's Technologies, Gent (Belgium)

Bright Light, Estugard

Musée de la Photographie, Charleroi

Himeji City Museum of Art, Himeji (Japan)

The Museum of Modern Art, Nigata

The Museum of Modern Art, Omiya

Images Fabriquées, Musée Sarret De Grozon, Arbois (France)

Europa – der Nacken des Stieres, Ubungsgelände auf dem Friedberg, Sulh

Retrospectives installations Vidéos, MUHKA, Antwerp

Review / Preview, Galerie Bugdahn und Kaimer, Düsseldorf

Philips Electronic Art, IFA, Berlin

Les choses et les mots, Galerie Thaddaeus Ropac, Paris

Kunst Verfremdet, Kulturhaus Dock 4, Kassel

Ieder kind is van marmer, Part 1, Bloom Gallery, Amsterdam

Ieder kind is van marmer, Part 2, Prinses Milhemina Bewaarschool, Amsterdam

I Am You, Odessa, Munique, Antwerp

1994   *Confrontation*, Musée d'Ixelles, Brussels

Multimédiale 3, HFG, Karlsruhe

Skulptur, Galerie Bugdahn und Kaimer, Düsseldorf

Depois de Amanhã / The Day After Tomorrow, Lisboa 94, Centro Cultural de Belém, Lisbon

---

OLAF METZEL

Born 1952, Berlin
Lives and works in Munich

SOLO EXHIBITIONS (SELECTION)

1982   Kunstraum München, Munich

1984   daad Galerie, Berlin

1985   Galerie Fahnemann, Berlin

1986   Michael Schwarz, Braunschweig

1989   Galerie Rudolf Zwirner, Cologne

1990   Produzenteugalerie, Hamburg

Westfälisches Landesmuseum für Kunst und Kulturgeschichte, Münster / Kunstraum, Munich

1991   Galerie Fahnemann, Berlin

1992   Kunstverein Braunschweig (with Ulrich Görlich)

Hamburger Kunsthalle, Hamburg

Staatliche Kunsthalle, Baden-Baden

GROUP EXHIBITIONS

1990   *The Readymade Boomerang*, 8th Biennale of Sydney

1991   *Umwandlungen*, National Museum of Contemporary Art Korea, Seul

Metropolis, Martin-Gropius-Bau, Berlin

Berlin Paris Bar, Artcurial, Paris

ars viva 91/92, Westfälischer Kunstverein, Münster, Museum Bochum u. a.

Dénonciation, Usine Fromage, Darnétal / Rouen

Das Goldene Zeitalter, Württembergischer Kunstverein, Stuttgard

Neues Museum Weserburg, Bremen

1992   *Sammlung Block,* Statens Museum for Kunst, Kopenhagen u. a.

1993   *Fontanelle - Kunst in (x) Zwischenfällen,* Kunstspeicher Potsdam

Übungsgelände, Suhl

Strange Hotel, Aarhus Kunstmuseum

1994   *Depois de Amanhã / The Day After Tomorrow,* Lisboa 94, Centro Cultural de Belém, Lisbon

---

CATHY DE MONCHAUX

Born 1960, London
Lives and works in London

SOLO EXHIBITIONS

1988   Mario Flecha Gallery, London

1990   Laure Genillard Gallery, London

Studio Guenzani, Milan

1991   Galerie Grita Insam, Vienna

Galerie Jennifer Flay, Paris

1993   Galerie Marc Jancou, Zurich

Studio Guenzani, Milan

Chisenhale Gallery, London

Centre for Contemporary Art, Glasgow

1994   Chisenhale Gallery, London

Arnolfini, Bristol

GROUP EXHIBITIONS (SELECTION)

1990   *The British Art Show 1990,* McLellan Gallery, Glasgow; Leeds City Art Gallery

Hayward Gallery, London

Je reviens de chez le charcutier, Galerie Ghislaine Hussenot, Paris

Laure Genillard Gallery, London

Visions go, Montreal

1991   *Plastic Fantastic Lover,* Blum Helman Warehouse, New York

1992   Kunsthalle Luzern, Lucerne

The Biennale of Sydney, Sydney

1993   Interzone, John Post Lee, New York

Recent British Sculpture, Arts Council of Great Britain (touring / Great Britain)

Prospect '93, Frankfurter Kunstverein, Frankfurt

In Site: New British Sculpture, Museum of Contemporary Art, Oslo; Ludwig Museum,
Budapest

1994   *Depois de Amanhã / The Day After Tomorrow,* Lisboa 94, Centro Cultural de Belém, Lisbon

---

MIGUEL PALMA

Born 1964, Lisbon
Lives and works in Lisbon

SOLO EXHIBITIONS

1988   *Periferia,* Biblioteca Nacional de Lisboa

1989   Galeria Quadrum, Lisbon

1991-2000   Projecto *Cemiterra-geraterra,* Jardins do Centro de Arte Moderna da Fundação
Calouste Gulbenkian, Lisbon

1992   *Ordem,* Galeria Quadrum, Lisbon

1993   *Olho Mágico,* Galeria Quadrum, Lisbon

Crash-Test, Galeria Quadrum, Lisbon

1994   *Engenho*, Átrio do Centro de Arte Moderna da Fundação Calouste Gulbenkian, Lisbon; Exponor (Salão do Automóvel), Oporto

GROUP EXHIBITIONS (SELECTION)

1993   *Arte Pública*, Galeria Quadrum, Lisbon

Imagens para os anos 90, Fundação de Serralves, Oporto; Centro de Exposições do Alto Tamega (Portugal)

1994   *Depois de Amanhã / The Day After Tomorrow*, Lisboa 94, Centro Cultural de Belém, Lisbon

---

JOÃO PENALVA

Born 1949, Lisbon
Lives and works in London

SOLO EXHIBITIONS

1983   Galeria Roma e Pavia, Oporto

Galeria de Arte Moderna, SNBA, Lisbon

1984   Cooperativa Árvore, Oporto

1987   Sala Atlântica, Galeria Nasoni, Oporto

1989   Francis Graham-Dixon Gallery, London

1990   Galeria Atlântica, Oporto

CAM / Fundação Calouste Gulbenkian, Lisbon

1991   Galeria Atlântica, Oporto

1992   Francis Graham-Dixon Gallery, London

1993   Galeria Atlântica, Oporto

GROUP EXHIBITIONS (SELECTION)

1990   *Works on Paper*, Francis Graham-Dixon Gallery, London

Four painters from London, Galeria Colégio de Arquitectos, Malaga

1991   *Gallery Artists*, Francis Graham-Dixon Gallery, London

1992   *Five Years*, Francis Graham-Dixon Gallery, London

Gallery Artists, Turske Hue-Williams, London

1993   *Recent British Painting — Arts Council Collection*, Royal Festival Hall (touring)

Coincidências, II Jornadas de Arte Contemporânea, Alfândega do Porto

1994   *Every Now and Then*, Rear Window at Richard Salmon Ltd., London

Depois de Amanhã / The Day After Tomorrow, Lisboa 94, Centro Cultural de Belém, Lisbon

COLLECTIONS

Arts Council of Great Britain (London); Caixa Geral de Depósitos (Lisbon); Centro de Arte Moderna / Fundação Calouste Gulbenkian (Lisbon); Museu Nacional de Arte Moderna / Casa de Serralves (Oporto).

MIGUEL ÂNGELO ROCHA

Born 1964, Lisboa
Lives and works in Lisbon

SOLO EXHIBITIONS

1991   Galeria Módulo, Lisbon

1992   Galeria Módulo, Lisbon

GROUP EXHIBITIONS (SELECTION)

1991   *Tendências*, Forum Picoas, Lisbon

Anos 90, Pré / Visões, SNBA, Lisbon

Arte com Timor, Palácio Galveias, Lisbon

1992   *Anos 90, Pré / Visões*, Palácio dos Duques, Guimarães (Portugal)

Bienal dos Jovens Criadores do Mediterrâneo, Valencia

Lusitânia — Identidade / Diversidade, Círculo de Belas Artes, Madrid

1993   *Imagens para os Anos 90*, Fundação de Serralves, Porto; Centro de Conferências do Alto Tâmega, Chaves (Portugal)

Previsões, Galeria Módulo, Oporto

1994   *Perspectives*, Centre d'Art Contemporain La Ferme du Buisson, Paris

Depois de Amanhã / The Day After Tomorrow, Lisboa 94, Centro Cultural de Belém, Lisbon

---

RUI SANCHES

Born 1954, Lisbon
Lives and works in Lisbon

SOLO EXHIBITIONS

1984   *Desenhos*, SNBA, Lisbon

Et in Arcadia Ego, etc., Galeria Diferença, Lisbon

1986   *Frágil*, Bar Frágil, Lisbon

1987   *Preto e Branco*, Galeria Diferença, Lisbon

1989   *A Marat*, Loja de Desenho, Lisboa

1990   *Alguns santos mártires e uma família pouco católica*, Galeria Atlântica, Oporto

Santos e fragmentos, Loja de Desenho, Lisbon

Capela dos túmulos, Convento de S. Francisco, Beja (Portugal)

1991   *Desenhos*, CAM / Fundação Calouste Gulbenkian, Lisbon

Galleria Stefania Miscetti, Rome

Galeria Cómicos / Luís Serpa, Lisbon

1992   *Body building*, Loja da Atalaia, Lisbon

Galeria Arco, Faro (Portugal)

1993   Chapelle de la Salpêtrière, Paris

Galeria J. M. Gomes Alves, Guimarães (Portugal)

Galeria Camargo Vilaça, S. Paulo

1994   *Corpos (e) móveis*, Galeria Cómicos / Luís Serpa, Lisbon

GROUP EXHIBITIONS (SELECTION)

1990   *Ultima Frontera - 7 artistes portuguesos*, Centro de Arte de Santa Mónica, Barcelona

Cabrita Reis, Rui Sanches, Fundación Luis Cernuda, Seville

De Verzameling II, Museum van Hedendaagse Kunst, Antwerp

PASTFUTURETENSE, Winnipeg Art Gallery e Vancouver Art Gallery (Canada)

1991   *De Europa*, Erice (Italy)

Sarmento, Chafes, Sanches, Galeria Diferença, Lisbon

Tríptico, Europália 91 — Portugal, Museum van Hedendaagse Kunst, Gent (Belgium)

1992   *Arte Contemporânea na Colecção FLAD*, CAM / Fundação Calouste Gulbenkian, Lisbon

Fundação de Serralves, Um Museu Português, Seville

10 Contemporâneos, Fundação de Serralves, Oporto

Silence to light, The Watari Museum of Contemporary Art, Tokyo

1993   *Tradición, Modernidad e Vangarda en el Seculo XX Português*, Auditorio de Galicia, Santiago de Compostela

Contemporary Art from Portugal: Western Lines, Hara Museum ARC, Tokyo

Cerco — BIO 93, Óbidos (Portugal)

1994   *Perspectives*, Centre d'Art Contemporain la Ferme du Bouisson, Noisiel (France)

Depois de Amanhã / The Day After Tomorrow, Lisboa 94, Centro Cultural de Belém, Lisbon

COLLECTIONS

Centro de Arte Moderna José de Azeredo Perdigão da Fundação Calouste Gulbenkian (Lisbon); Fundação de Serralves (Oporto); Fundação Luso-Americana para o Desenvolvimento (Lisbon); Caixa Geral de Depósitos (Lisbon); Museum van Hedendaagse Kunst (Antwerp); several private collections.

JULIÃO SARMENTO

Born 1948, Lisbon
Lives and works in Sintra (Portugal)

SOLO EXHIBITIONS (SELECTION)

1982   *Pinturas em Papel*, ARTA, Lisbon

Drawings, Galerie Erika + Otto Friedrich, Bern

Pinturas 1981/82, Casa de Bocage, Setúbal (Portugal)

1984   Galeria Juana de Aizpuru, Madrid

Pinturas, Galeria Cómicos, Lisbon

Arbeiten auf Papier, Galerie Erika + Otto Friedrich, Bern

1985   *Perspective 85*, Art 16'85, Basel

Galeria Cómicos, Lisbon

1986   Galerie Heinrich Ehrhardt, Frankfurt

Galleria Marilena Bonomo, Bari

Anders Tornberg Gallery, Lund

Museo de Belas Artes de Malaga

Neue Arbeiten, Galerie Bernd Klüser, Munich

1987   Galeria Marga Paz, Madrid

1988   Galerie Erika + Otto Friedrich, Bern

Galleria Giorgio Persano, Turin

Gnadenstoss, Galerie Bernd Klüser, Munich

1989   Galeria Cómicos, Lisbon

Xavier Hufkens, Brussels

Galeria Marga Paz, Madrid

1990   Galleria Giorgio Persano, Milan

Neue Arbeiten, Galerie Bernd Klüser, Munich

Dias de Escuro e de Luz, Galeria Pedro Oliveira, Oporto

Fundación Luis Cernuda, Seville

Galerie Montenay, Paris

Louver Gallery, New York

Witte de With, Center for Contemporary Art, Rotterdam

Pinturas Brancas, Galeria Cómicos / Luís Serpa, Lisbon

1992   Xavier Hufkens, Brussels

Fundação de Serralves, Oporto

Galerie Erika + Otto Friedrich, Bern

Galeria Luisa Strina, S. Paulo

1993   Centro de Arte Moderna, Fundação Calouste Gulbenkian, Lisbon

Metalúrgica Alentejana (com Juan Muñoz), Beja (Portugal)

1994   *The White Paintings*, Centre des Arts Saidye Bronfman, Montreal

IVAM, Centre del Carme, Valencia

Laura and Alice, Galerie Bernd Klüser, Munich

Ruth Bloom Gallery, Santa Monica, California

GROUP EXHIBITIONS (SELECTION)

1990 *Vom Haben und vom Wollen Perspektiven für eine Staatsgalerie moderner Kunst Eine Ausstellung*, Staatsgalerie moderner Kunst, Haus der Kunst, Munich

1991 *Metropolis*, Martin-Gropius-Bau, Berlin

Tríptico, Europália 91 — Portugal, Museum van Hedendaagse Kunst, Gent (Belgium)

1992 *Regard Multiple*, Centre Georges Pompidou, Paris

Arte Amazonas, Museu de Arte Moderna, Rio de Janeiro

Museu de Arte, Brasilia

Bienal de S. Paulo, Parque Ibirapuera

Portugisisk Nutidskunst — Rego, Sanches, Sarmento, Vejle Kunstmuseum, Vejle

10 Contemporâneos, Fundação de Serralves, Oporto

Der Gefrorene Leopard, Galerie Bernd Klüser, Munich

Terrae Motus alla Reggia di Caserta, Palazzo Reale di Caserta, Caserta

1993 *The Brushstroke: Painting in the 90's*, Ruth Bloom Gallery, Santa Monica, California

Klima Global — Arte Amazonas, Staatliche Kunsthalle, Berlin; Technische Sammlungen der Stadt Dresden, Dresden; Ludwig Forum für Internationale Kunst, Aachen

Contemporary Art from Portugal: Western Lines, Hara Museum ARC, Shibukawa

Cerco — BIO'93, Solar de Santa Maria, Óbidos (Portugal)

1994 *Four Europeans: Helmut Dorner, Lili Dujourie, Harald Klingelholler, Julião Sarmento*, Laura Carpenter Fine Art, Santa Fe, New Mexico

Unbound: Possibilities in Painting, Hayward Gallery, London

Depois de Amanhã / The Day After Tomorrow, Lisboa 94, Centro Cultural de Belém, Lisbon

COLLECTIONS

Caixa Geral de Depósitos (Lisbon); Centro Cultural de Belém (Lisbon); Centro de Arte Moderna / Fundação Calouste Gulbenkian (Lisbon); Fondazione Amelio (Naples); Fondo Artistico dello Archivio Storico delle Arti Contemporanee della Biennale di Venezia (Venice); Fundação das Descobertas (Lisbon); Fundação de Serralves (Oporto); Fundação Luso-Americana para o Desenvolvimento (Lisbon); Galerija Grada (Zagreb); Hara Museum of Contemporary Art (Tokyo); Liechtensteinische Staatliche Kunstsammlung (Liechtenstein); Malmö Museum (Malmö); Ministério das Finanças (Lisbon); Moderna Museet (Stockholm); Museo Español de Arte Contemporáneo (Madrid); Museu d'Art Contemporani Barcelona (Barcelona); Museum van Hedendaagse Kunst (Antwerp); Museum van Hedendaagse Kunst (Gent); Musée National d'Art Moderne / Centre Georges Pompidou (Paris); Secretaria de Estado da Cultura (Lisbon); Staatsgalerie Moderner Kunst (Munich); Stadt Museet (Lund); Städtische Galerie am Markt (Schwäbisch Hall); Städtische Galerie im Lenbachhaus (Munich); Städtische Galerie (Erlangen); Tel Aviv Museum of Art (Tel Aviv); The Saison Foundation / The Museum of Modern Art (Takanawa).

FRANK THIEL

Born 1966, Kleinmachnow (Germany)
Lives and works in Berlin

SOLO EXHIBITIONS

1991 Galerie Zellermeyer, Berlin

1992 Galerie Zellermayer, Berlin

1993 Galeria Módulo, Lisbon

GROUP EXHIBITIONS (SELECTION)

1990   Encontros Internacionais de Fotografia, Arles

1991   *Panorama des Panoramas,* Centre National de la Photographie, Palais de Tokyo, Paris

        Interferenzen — Kunst aus Westberlin 1960-1990 Riga

        Galerie Zellermayer, Berlin

        Neue Aspekte, Berlinische Galerie, Berlin

1992   *Einsamkeit — A German Sensation,* Veruela de Moncayo + Fundacion La Caixa, Madrid

        and Barcelona

        Galerie Zellermayer, Berlin

        Jahreslabor, Photostipendiaten, Berlinische Galerie, Berlin

        Humpty Dumpty's Caleidoscope — a new generation of german artists, Museum of

        Contemporary Art, Sydney

1993   *Einsamkeit — A German Sensation,*Casal Solleric, Palma de Maiorca

        Emigration — Bilder von Abschied, Reise, Tod, Galerie Mosel und Tschechow, Munich

        Galerie Zellermayer, Berlin

1994   *Diario,* Museu de Arte Moderna, Rio de Janeiro; Galerie Hohenthal und Bergen, Cologne

        Depois de Amanhã / The Day After Tomorrow, Lisboa 94, Centro Cultural de Belém, Lisbon

---

BALTAZAR TORRES

Born 1961, Figueira de Castelo Rodrigo (Portugal)
Lives and works in Portimão (Portugal)

SOLO EXHIBITIONS

1990   Galeria Módulo, Oporto

        Galeria Módulo, Lisbon

        Galeria J. M. Gomes Alves, Guimarães (Portugal)

1991   Galeria Módulo, Lisbon

        Biblioteca Nacional, Lisbon

1994   Centro de Artes Plásticas, Coimbra (Portugal)

GROUP EXHIBITIONS (SELECTION)

1990   *Sommer Inspiration,* Hanover

1991   *Momentos da Arte Contemporânea I: Anos 90 Pré/Visões,* SNBA, Lisbon

        Risco, Europália 91 — Portugal, Gand

1992   Encontro de Arte Jovem, Chaves (Portugal)

1993   *Imagens para os Anos 90,* Fundação de Serralves, Oporto

1994   *Depois de Amanhã / The Day After Tomorrow,* Lisboa 94, Centro Cultural de Belém, Lisbon

---

JAMES TURRELL

Born 1943, Los Angeles
Lives and works in Flagstaff (Arizona,)

SOLO EXHIBITIONS

1967   Pasadena Art Museum, Pasadena, California

1968   Main and Hill Studio, Santa Monica, California

1969   Main and Hill Studio, Santa Monica, California

1970   Main and Hill Studio, Santa Monica, California

1976   Stedelijk Museum, Amsterdam

        ARCO Center for Visual Art, Los Angeles

1977   Heiner Friedrich Gallery, Cologne

1980   Herron Gallery, Herron School of Art, Indianapolis

University of Arizona Museum of Art, Tucson, Arizona

Whitney Museum of American Art, New York

1981 Leo Castelli Gallery, New York

Portland Center for Visual Arts, Portland, Oregon

1982 Center for Contemporary Art, Seattle

1983 Israel Museum, Jesuralem

Hayden Gallery, Massachusetts Institute of Technology, Boston

Flow Ace Gallery, Venice, California

Mattress Factory, Pittsburg, Pennsylvania

University of Delaware Art Gallery, Newark, Delaware

Musée d'Art Moderne de la Ville de Paris, Paris

1984 Flow Ace Gallery, Los Angeles

Capp Street Project, San Francisco

Marian Locks Gallery, Philadelphia

1985 Bernard Jacobson Gallery, Los Angeles

Marian Goodman Gallery, New York

Roger Ramsay Gallery, Chicago

Karl Bornstein Gallery, Santa Monica, California

Museum of Contemporary Art, Los Angeles

1986 University of Arizona Museum of Art, Tucson, Arizona

Marian Goodman Gallery, New York

P. S. 1, Long Island City, New York (permanent installation)

Center for Contemporary Arts, Santa Fe, New Mexico

1987 Yvon Lambert Galerie, Paris

Phoenix Art Museum, Phoenix, Arizona

Kunsthalle, Basel

University Art Gallery, University of California, Riverside, California

1988 Lannan Museum, Lakeworth, Florida

Roger Ramsay Gallery, Chicago

Center for Contemporary Arts, Santa Fe, New Mexico (permanent piece)

Coconino Center for the Arts, Flagstaff, Arizona

Museum of Northern Arizona, Flagstaff, Arizona

Jean Bernier Gallery, Athens

1989 Florida State University Gallery and Museum, Tallahassee, Florida

Security Pacific Gallery, Costa Mesa, California

Musée des Beaux-Arts de Nimes, Nimes

1990 Galerie Froment and Putman, Paris

Newport Harbor Art Museum, Newport Beach, California

Boulder Art Center, Boulder, Colorado

Stein-Gladstone Gallery, New York

P. S. 1, Long Island City, New York

La Jolla Museum of Contemporary Art, La Jolla, California

Museum of Modern Art, New York

Stuart Regan Gallery, Los Angeles

Turske & Turske, Zurich

1991	Kunstmuseum, Berna
	Rhode Island School of Design, Providence, Rhode Island
	Williams College Art Museum, Williamstown, Massachusetts
	Indianapolis Museum of Art, Indianapolis (permanent installation)
	Galerie Froment and Putman, Paris
	Lisa Sette Gallery, Scottsdale, Arizona
	Friedman and Guinness Gallery, Frankfurt
	Confort Modern, Poitiers
	Turske & Turske, Zurich
	Universidad Internacional Menedez y Pelayo, Santander
	The Principal Corporation, Des Moines, Iowa (permanent installation)
	Anthony d'Offay Gallery, London
	Centro Cultural Arte Contempaneo, Mexico City (permanent installation)
	Carpenter Center, Harvard University, Cambridge, Massachusetts
	Turske & Turske, Zurich
1992	Musée d'Art Contemporain, Lyon
	Isy Brachot Gallery, Brussels
	Gallery Cora Holzl, Düsseldorf
	Kunstsammlung fur Nordrhein und Westphalen, Düsseldorf
	Kunstverein, Düsseldorf
	Sprengel Museum, Hanover (permanent installation)
	Stroom, The Hague, Holland
	Turske Hue-Williams, London
	Confort Moderne, Poitiers
	Wiener Secession, Vienna
	Fundacio Espai Poblenou, Barcelona (permanent installation)
	Belvedere, Royal Gardens of Prague Castel, Prag
	Claremont / Pitzer Colleges, Claremont, California
	Weisser Raum, Hamburg
	Henry Art Gallery, Seattle
	Fuel Gallery, Seattle
	The Israel Museum, Jerusalem
	Fundacion La Caixa, Madrid
	Lenbachhaus, Munich
1993	Ace Gallery, Los Angeles
	Hayward Gallery, London
	Anthony d'Offay Gallery, London
	Butler Gallery, Kilkenny, Irland
	Institute of Contemporary Art, Philadelphia
	Marian Locks Gallery, Philadelphia
	Henry Moore Sculpture Trust, Halifax (England)
	Knoedler Gallery, New York
1994	Barbara Gladstone Gallery, New York
	Lisa Sette Gallery, Scottsdale, Arizona
	Galeria de Elvira Gonzales, Madrid

Museum of Modern Art, New York

Crawford Municipal Art Gallery, Cork, (Irland)

American Center, Paris

Paris Opera, Atelier Theatre & Music, Nanterre

GROUP EXHIBITIONS (SELECTION)

1990   Kupfer Druck, Peter Kneubuhler, Zurich

Israel Museum International Council Program, The Israel Museum, Jerusalem

Fondation Cartier pour l'Art Contemporain, Jouy-en-Josas, (France)

Château de Rochechouart, Musée Departamental, Rochechouart, (France)

La Jolla Museum of Contemporary Art, La Jolla, California

Le Musée d'Art Contemporain de Montreal, Montreal

Un Choix d'Art Minimal dans la Collection Panza, Musée d'Art Moderne de la

Ville de Paris, Paris

Espace Electra, Paris

Karl Bornstein Gallery, Santa Monica, California

Turske & Turske, Zurich

1991   Dalsheimer Gallery, Baltimore

Museum of Contemporary Art, Los Angeles

Espace Lulay, Liège

Indianapolis Museum of Art, Indianapolis

Museum für Moderne Kunst, Frankfurt

Katonah Museum of Art, Katonah, New York

Galerie Cora Holzl, Düsseldorf

Turske & Turske, Zurich

Whitney Museum at Equitable Center, New York

Reynolds / Minor Gallery, Richmond, Virginia

Schwerelos, Berlin

1992   Stein Gladstone, New York

Geneve Musée d'Art et d'Histoire, Geneva

Kunsthalle, Basel

De Pont Foundation, Tilburg (Holland)

Santa Monica Museum of Art, Santa Monica, California

Galerie Froment Putman, Paris

1993   *Mediale*, Kunsthalle, Hamburg

Amerikanische Kunst Im 20 Jahrhundert, Martin-Gropius Bau, Berlin

Azure, Fondation Cartier pour l'Art Contemporain, Jouy-en-Josas, (France)

Differentes Natures, La Défense, Paris

Biennale d'Art Contemporaine, Lyon

American Art of the 20th Century, Royal Academy of Art, London

Galerie Joan Prats, Barcelona

1994   *L'architecte est sur les lieux collections du FRAC Centre*, Musée des Beaux-Arts de Chartres,

Chartres (France)

Lannan Foundation, Los Angeles

Landscape as Metaphor, Denver Art Museum, Denver

Depois de Amanhã / The Day After Tomorrow, Lisboa 94, Centro Cultural de Belém, Lisbon

COLLECTIONS

(Installations)

Center for Contemporary Arts (Santa Fe, New Mexico); Centro Cultural Arte Contempaneo (Mexico City); Château De Rochechouart (Rochechouart, France); Chicago Art Institute (Chicago); De Pont Stitching Foundation (Tilburg, Holland); Fundacion La Caixa (Madrid); Fundacio Espai Poblenou (Barcelona); Fondation Cartier pour l'Art Contemporain (Paris); Guggenheim Museum (New York); Indianapolis Art Museum (Indianapolis); Israel Museum (Jerusalem); Kunstsammlung für Nordheim und Westfalen (Düsseldorf); San Diego Museum of Contemporary Art (La Jolla, California); Le Musée d'Art Contemporain de Montreal (Montreal); Lenbachhaus (Munich); Mattress Factory (Pittsburg); Ministère de la Culture (Paris); Musée d'Art Contemporain (Lyon); Museum für Moderne Kunst (Frankfurt); Museum of Contemporary Art (Los Angeles); Museum of Modern Art (New York); Newport Harbor Art Museum (Newport); Panza Collection (Varese); Principal Corporation (Des Moines, Iowa); P. S. I (Long Island City, New York); San Francisco Museum of Modern Art (San Francisco); Seattle Art Museum (Seattle); Sprengel Museum (Hanover); Stroom (Den Haag, Holland); Whitney Museum of American Art (New York).

(Graphics)

Bank of America (San Francisco); Brooklyn Museum (New York); Chase Manhattan Bank (New York); Dallas Museum (Dallas); Dia Art Foundation (New York); Fogg Art Museum (Cambridge, Massachusetts); Guggenheim Museum (New York); Humanities Researche Center (Austin, Texas); Israel Museum (Jerusalem); Lannan Foundation (Los Angeles); Marian Koogler McNay Art Institute (San Antonio, Texas); Menil Foundation (Houston); Moderna Museet (Stockholm); New York Public Library (New York); Philadelphia Museum of Art (Philadelphia); Prudential Insurance of America (Newark, New Jersey); Skystone Foundation (Flagstaff, Arizona); Smith College Museum of Art (Northampton, Massachusetts); Sprengle Museum (Hanover); Stedelijk Museum (Amsterdam); Walker Art Center (Minneapolis).

XANA

Born 1959, Lisbon
Lives and works in Lagos (Portugal)

SOLO EXHIBITIONS

1985   *From Crocodile Islands*, Galeria Diferença, Lisbon
1986   Galeria Módulo, Lisbon
1987   Galeria Módulo, Oporto
1988   *Raspar as Palavras*, Loja de Desenho, Lisbon
         Ursos e Flores, do Moderno ao Neo-Neo, Galeria de Colares
1989   Galeria Valentim de Carvalho, Lisbon
1990   Galeria Valentim de Carvalho, Lisbon
         Cooperativa Árvore, Oporto
1991   *Arte Opaca (Unidimensional) Atípica*, Galeria A5, Santo Tirso (Portugal)
1992   Kunstlerhaus Mousonturm, Frankfurt
1993   *Super Plástica*, Galeria Valentim de Carvalho, Lisbon
1994   *Pinturas Quase Planas*, Galeria Évora-Arte, Évora (Portugal)

INSTALLATIONS

1987   *Alvos* (intervention at the Fortaleza), Festival de Sagres, Sagres (Portugal)

1991   *Quatro Esculturas*, Cidade Universitária, Festas de Lisboa, Lisbon

    Intervenção em Quatro Edifícios de Osnabruck, Arte Portuguesa 1992, Osnabruck

1992   *Intervenção no Metropolitano*, Festas de Lisboa, Lisbon

1993   *Amor Trabalho Sabedoria*, Jornadas de Arte Contemporânea, Oporto

SET DESIGN

1988   *O Lagarto do Âmbar* de M. Estela Guedes, Acarte, Fundação Calouste Gulbenkian, Lisbon

1992   *Diving* (sceneries and props), coreografia de Rui Horta, Soap Dance Theatre, Frankfurt

GROUP EXHIBITIONS (SELECTION)

1991   *Arte com Timor*, Palácio Galveias, Lisbon

1992   *Arte Contemporânea Portuguesa na Colecção da Fundação Luso-Americana
    para o Desenvolvimento*, CAM / Fundação Calouste Gulbenkian, Lisbon

    Muestra de Pintura y Grabado Portugueses Contemporáneos, Museo de Huelva

    Bravo — Reencontros, Galeria Alda Cortez, Lisbon

1993   *Tradición, Modernidad e Vangarda en el Século XX Portugués*, Auditorio de Galicia,
    Santiago de Compostela

    Ilegítimos, Jóias Portuguesas Contemporâneas 1993, Artefacto 3, Lisbon

1994   *Ilegítimos*, The George Washington University, Washington, e Galerie Hilde Leiss,
    Hamburg

    Quando o mundo nos cai em cima, Centro Cultural de Belém, Lisbon

    WX (com Marta Wengorovius), Blanca de Navarra / Centro Cultural de Lisbon,
    Madrid

    Desenhos Contemporâneos, Lisboa 94, Sala do Risco, Lisbon

    Depois de Amanhã / The Day After Tomorrow, Lisboa 94, Centro Cultural de Belém, Lisbon

COLLECTIONS

Centro de Arte Moderna / Fundação Calouste Gulbenkian (Lisbon); Fundação de Serralves
(Oporto); Secretaria de Estado da Cultura (Lisbon); Fundação Luso-Americana para o
Desenvolvimento (Lisbon); Caixa Geral de Depósitos (Lisbon).